World War I for Teens

An Enthralling Guide to the Conflict that Redefined Nations

© Copyright 2025 - All rights reserved.

The content contained within this book may not be reproduced, duplicated, or transmitted without direct written permission from the author or the publisher.

Under no circumstances will any blame or legal responsibility be held against the publisher, or author, for any damages, reparation, or monetary loss due to the information contained within this book, either directly or indirectly.

Legal Notice:

This book is copyright protected. It is only for personal use. You cannot amend, distribute, sell, use, quote, or paraphrase any part, or the content within this book, without the consent of the author or publisher.

Disclaimer Notice:

Please note the information contained within this document is for educational and entertainment purposes only. All effort has been executed to present accurate, up-to-date, reliable, and complete information. No warranties of any kind are declared or implied. Readers acknowledge that the author is not engaging in the rendering of legal, financial, medical, or professional advice. The content within this book has been derived from various sources. Please consult a licensed professional before attempting any techniques outlined in this book.

By reading this document, the reader agrees that under no circumstances is the author responsible for any losses, direct or indirect, that are incurred as a result of the use of the information contained within this document, including, but not limited to, errors, omissions, or inaccuracies.

Free limited time bonus

Stop for a moment. We have a free bonus set up for you. The problem is this: we forget 90% of everything that we read after 7 days. Crazy fact, right? Here's the solution: we've created a printable, 1-page pdf summary for this book that you're reading now. All you have to do to get your free pdf summary is to go to the following website: https://livetolearn.lpages.co/enthrallinghistory/

Or, Scan the QR code!

Once you do, it will be intuitive. Enjoy, and thank you!

Table of Contents

INTRODUCTION 1
CHAPTER 1: EUROPE BEFORE THE STORM 3
CHAPTER 2: AN ASSASSINATION IN SARAJEVO 15
CHAPTER 3: LIFE IN THE TRENCHES 28
CHAPTER 4: THE KEY BATTLES OF WORLD WAR I 40
CHAPTER 5: THE FORGOTTEN FRONTS..52
CHAPTER 6: THE TECHNOLOGY OF WORLD WAR I 64
CHAPTER 7: THE UNITED STATES ENTERS THE FRAY 78
CHAPTER 8: REVOLUTION AND THE END OF THE WAR 90
CHAPTER 9: THE TREATIES: A NEW MAP OF EUROPE AND THE WORLD 101
CONCLUSION 110
ANSWERS 114
HERE'S ANOTHER BOOK BY ENTHRALLING HISTORY THAT YOU MIGHT LIKE...120
FREE LIMITED TIME BONUS..121
BIBLIOGRAPHY 122
IMAGE SOURCES 124

Introduction

It was "the war to end all wars," or so they said. British author H. G. Wells wrote that this war would be history's most pivotal conflict. It would usher in a new world order of peace. No one would need armies because there would be no more wars. He was wrong. Only two decades later, World War II exploded on the scene as human history's most lethal war of all time.

This engaging, easy-to-read book dives into the drama and deadly technology that drove World War I from 1914 to 1918. How did the murder of a love-struck couple spark the war? Why were nations on the other side of the planet dragged into a local conflict? What was it like for the soldiers living in muddy trenches for months on end? How did chemical weapons play a horrible role? What happened when the Communist revolution upended Russia?

This book introduces the major players and their bizarre stories. The primary forces were the Central Powers (Austria-Hungary, the Ottoman Empire, and Germany) fighting against the Allied Powers (France, Britain, and Russia). Yet, before the war ended, it sucked in over thirty nations. Never had so many countries been at war.

When the war began, folks thought it would be over in months. Instead, four nightmarish years passed before the war ended. The root causes of WWI spread their tentacles back over a century. The war still affects today's world, especially Southeastern Europe's Balkan nations. In fact, that was where it all began. Two shots from a teenage assassin's pistol plunged every continent except Antarctica into war.

World War I's lasting impact is why reading history is essential. We learn how we got to this point and why things are how they are. It teaches us how to avoid history repeating itself. On the other hand, history also inspires us with the stories of brave and clever people who improved the world.

Bullets, bombs, and poison gas killed at least sixteen million people in WWI, more than any other war up to that time. World War I unleashed spine-chilling new technology, like tanks, military aircraft with machine guns, and chemical warfare. Yet it also introduced mind-blowing manufacturing and communications advances that changed the course of human history.

World War I redesigned the world map and redefined nations. When the misguided efforts of Europe's rulers failed to defuse a crisis, the war began. By the war's end, the mighty Ottoman, Austria-Hungary, and Russian empires had cratered. Emperors and kings toppled from their thrones as the boundaries of countries were rearranged. World War I introduced novel political ideology, social norms, and morality.

This book highlights the heroes of the war, including brilliant generals and the millions of men and teens slogging it out in the trenches. Women heroically ran factories and farms at home and manned communications near the front lines. And let's not forget the horses, mules, dogs, and pigeons that played their part. We will unwrap their stories and more!

Chapter 1: Europe Before the Storm

How did World War I start? To answer that question, we need to understand the complex geopolitical landscape in Europe leading up to the war. How did shifting alliances and earlier wars among great and lesser powers play a part? What events escalated the descent into war? What was the Black Hand, and how did this terrorist group in an obscure country trigger a war that encircled the globe?

Who Were the Major Players and Key Alliances?

At the beginning of the war, the major players were Austria-Hungary and Germany against Russia and France. Tangled alliances brought other countries, like Britain and the United States, into the war. Some European countries, like Belgium and Luxembourg, declared they were neutral. They did not want to get involved. Unfortunately, they were inconveniently located between Germany and France. Germany ignored their neutrality and ripped through their countries to attack France.

In the early 1900s, Europe's six powerful empires were in one of two alliances: the *Triple Entente* (pronounced aan-**taant**) and the *Triple Alliance*. In 1882, Austria-Hungary, Germany, and Italy formed the Triple Alliance because they feared Russia or France might attack one of them. They promised each other they would help if any of the three got attacked. France, Britain, and Russia were all worried about Germany attacking them. The Triple Alliance made them even more concerned. In 1904, France and Britain signed the *Entente Cordiale* (kor-dyal), which means "warm agreement or friendship" in French. Russia joined the Entente in 1907.

The Triple Alliance (Germany, Austria-Hungary, and Italy) and the Triple Entente (Britain, France, and Russia) [1]

What Is Imperialism? How Did It Come into Play among the European Powers?

Imperialism is when one country controls other countries. A country that controls one or more other countries is an *empire*. All the countries involved in the Triple Alliance and Triple Entente were empires. All the Triple Alliance and Triple Entente nations—except Britain—wanted to expand in Europe. This meant taking over other countries, especially the poorer and weaker nations. Austria and Hungary joined to form an empire that extended into southeastern Europe's Balkan states.

The *Age of Imperialism* began around 1880 as European countries competed for colonies. Britain, France, Italy, and Germany had colonies outside Europe. Russia's empire extended into today's Central Asian countries of Uzbekistan, Kazakhstan, Turkmenistan, Kyrgyzstan, and Tajikistan.

Belgium, Britain, France, Germany, Italy, Portugal, and Spain joined the *Scramble for Africa*. They divided Africa into colonies so they could help themselves to its natural resources, like diamonds, gold, rubber, and timber.

These powers also wanted to protect trade routes and have safe ports. The fastest way to sail from Europe to East Asia was through Egypt's Suez Canal (completed in 1869). The other way was to sail around the bottom of Africa. Both required friendly ports for ships. Thus, the Scramble for Africa involved exploiting natural resources and protecting trade with East Asia.

What Were the Moroccan Crises?

In 1905, Germany's emperor, Kaiser Wilhelm II, visited the country of Morocco in North Africa. At the time, France had a powerful influence on Morocco. Britain and Spain had signed a secret agreement in 1904 with France, giving their blessing for France to establish a *"protectorate"* over Morocco. (A protectorate is when a strong country protects and partly controls a weaker country. In theory, the weak country still has its own government, but the "protector" controls things like the economy and foreign policy.)

Since Spain was only nine miles across the Strait of Gibraltar from Morocco, it already had a protectorate in place for the Morocco side of the Strait of Gibraltar, which it would keep. France and Spain wanted to collect customs fees and protect Morocco's ports. Part of the secret agreement was that Spain would eventually annex Morocco's coast directly across from Spain. France, Britain, and Spain believed Morocco needed reforms in its administration, finances, and military.

Kaiser Wilhelm of Germany ruffled feathers in Europe when he gave a speech in Morocco in 1905. "The sultan of Morocco is the ruler of a free country!" he declared. "He is not under foreign control!"

Kaiser Wilhelm II in Tangier, Morocco, 1905 [2]

Wilhelm wanted to shake things up in Morocco. He also wanted Germany to have a piece of Morocco's lucrative trade. He was challenging France's role in Morocco and testing the Triple Entente. France's people reacted in anger. However, their premier, Maurice Rouvier, tried to solve the problem without provoking war. He agreed to a conference with Germany, yet he also moved his troops to the border of France and Germany.

Thirteen nations attended the Algeciras Conference of 1906. Only Austria-Hungary supported Germany. Britain, Italy, Spain, Russia, and the United States all supported France. Germany had no choice but to agree to France's protectorate over Morocco. The First Moroccan Crisis was over.

Nevertheless, five years later, Germany was stirring up trouble again. The Agadir Crisis, or the Second Moroccan Crisis, erupted in July 1911 when Germany deployed a warship, the SMS *Panther*, to Morocco's port of Agadir. The German excuse was that the Moroccans were protesting French rule. They were there to "keep the peace."

Germany was still bitter that France was allowed to have a protectorate over Morocco. "If we accept this, what do we get?" the Germans said. The French rolled their eyes. "We've got to give Germany something, or they'll never leave us in peace!"

Consequently, the French and Germans started negotiating. After four months, they finally came to an agreement in November 1911. Germany accepted France's protectorate over Morocco. In return, Germany got territory in the French colony of Congo (today's Republic of Congo). France's protectorate over Morocco officially began in March 1912, ending Moroccan independence. Despite friendly negotiations, the divide between France and Germany contributed to World War I.

What Was the Arms Race All About?

As the Moroccan crises were playing out, Britain identified Germany as its number one foreign threat. Perhaps more alarming than the Moroccan affair was that Germany was building a vast battle fleet. Up to this time, Britain had ruled the seas with its Royal Navy, the world's largest and most intimidating war fleet. Since Great Britain was an island kingdom, it needed to protect itself from invasion. It also needed to protect its merchant ships sailing around the world, as Britain's economy had always depended on sea trade.

In 1898, Germany started building its naval fleet, beginning a watery arms race with Britain. An **arms race** is a competition between countries for weapon superiority. It includes the type of weapons, how lethal they are, and how many a country has. In this case, Germany was competing with Britain for the most warships and the deadliest weapons on them. Britain already had a naval fleet, so at first, Germany was just trying to catch up. That's when Britain took the competition up a notch.

Twin guns on the HMS Dreadnought [3]

In 1906, Britain began building the **dreadnought**—a new and terrifying battleship. It was the first navy ship to use a steam turbine engine. A **turbine engine** has something like fan blades, and high-pressure steam spins the blades. The rotational energy from the turbine turns a propeller shaft that pushes the ship forward. The HMS *Dreadnought* was Britain's first ship with the dreadnought design.

With a top speed of twenty-one knots (twenty-four miles per hour), the HMS *Dreadnought* was the fastest battleship in the world. She had ten guns that were twelve inches in diameter. They were mounted in twin turrets with rotating gun houses that protected the crew as they loaded the guns. The guns shot 850-pound shells that flew for fourteen miles, exploding on impact. During WWI in 1915, the HMS *Dreadnought* rammed and sank the SM *U-29*, a German U-boat. It was the only time a battleship sunk a submarine.

Germany decided it couldn't compete with England's battleships, so it focused on submarines. Instead of engaging warships or British submarines during WWI, it attacked merchant ships carrying food and supplies to Great Britain. Most German submarines were U-boats that depended on battery power when underwater, limiting how long they could stay under the surface. Unlike modern submarines, they mostly sailed on the surface using fuel engines, only diving to evade the enemy or launch an attack. By the beginning of WWI, Germany had built a fleet of forty-eight submarines.

How Did Events in Bosnia and Serbia Escalate the Conflict?

The Balkan region of Southeastern Europe was the continent's most unstable region in the early twentieth century. It's still unstable today. There, ethnic groups in several small countries violently vied for control. They had been at each other's throats for over a century. Each group felt it had the right to expand, even if that meant displacing the others. All the groups were South Slavic, but they were divided by religion and language. The Serbs spoke Serbian and were mainly Christian Orthodox, while the primarily Muslim Bosniaks spoke the Bosnian language. The Croats were mainly Roman Catholic and spoke Croatian.

Balkan states before WWI (English labels added) '

Borders did not define these ethnic groups. For instance, Serbia was a tiny country, roughly in the same place it is today, north of Greece and Macedonia. Its people were mostly Serbs, but it was also home to Hungarians, Bosniaks, and other groups. Serbia's next-door neighbor was Bosnia-Herzegovina. Bosnia had Bosniaks, Croats, and Serbs. Tensions between these ethnic and religious groups often boiled over.

The conflict didn't only involve these ethnic groups. Several extensive empires, like the Ottoman Empire, Russia, and Austria-Hungary, tried to control the Balkan states.

The Ottoman Turks were not European. They were originally from Central Asia and migrated to Turkey in the thirteenth century. In 1453, they conquered Constantinople, which sits on the narrow strip of land between the Marmara and Black seas where Europe meets Asia. It had been the capital of the Greek Byzantine Empire. The Turks renamed it Istanbul and made it their capital.

In 1459, the Turks grabbed part of Serbia. Four years later, they conquered Bosnia. Under Suleiman the Magnificent, the Ottoman Empire swallowed the Middle East in the 1500s. This Islamic empire also conquered parts of Bulgaria, Greece, Hungary, Macedonia, and Romania.

In 1804, the Ottomans who ruled Serbia were on bad terms with their sultan in Istanbul. They were afraid the sultan would use the Serbs against them. To strike fear in the Serbs, the Turks chopped off the heads of the Serbian leaders. This move backfired. It triggered the Serbian Revolution, in which the Serbs declared themselves an independent state with Russia's support.

However, France invaded Russia in 1812, and when Russia was distracted, the Ottomans took advantage and grabbed Serbia back. They massacred hundreds of Serbs and sold thousands into slavery. In the 1870s, war broke out between Russia and the Ottoman Empire. The Serbs fought on the Russian side and carved out their tiny kingdom in the rugged mountains. Serbia annexed neighboring Bosnia despite Serbians only being a minority of Bosnia's population. Bosnia also technically belonged to Austria. However, Serbia was landlocked, and Bosnia gave them access to the Adriatic Sea, which they desperately wanted for sea trade.

In 1903, Serbia's king became friendly with Austria, which enraged his people. The Serbian army officers shot their king and queen, threw their bodies out the palace window, and installed a new king loyal to Russia. Being a royal in Europe was a dangerous occupation! The reason the Serbs killed their king was that Austria and Hungary had formed a two-state empire. They feared that Austria-Hungary would invade the Balkans, and they were right.

In 1908, Austria-Hungary scooped up Bosnia and its tiny neighbor, Herzegovina, into its empire. The Serbs were outraged because they felt like they owned Bosnia. They turned to their old friends, the Russians, for help. However, Russia had its own problems. It had just suffered a crushing and humiliating loss in its war with Japan for control of Korea and Manchuria (the part of northeastern China next to Korea). Its army and navy were in disarray, and most of its people lived in severe poverty. If the Serbs wanted to take Bosnia, they would have to do it on their own.

Members of the Black Hand [5]

What Was the Black Hand?

The same Serbian army officers who murdered their king and queen formed a secret society in 1911 that folks nicknamed the **Black Hand**. Its official name was *Unification or Death*, and it was a military organization. Its goal was to use any means necessary, including terrorism, to liberate the Serbs outside Serbia who were still under the

Ottoman Empire or Austria-Hungary. They wanted to create a "Greater Serbia."

The Black Hand's focus was Bosnia, where it had a network of cells. Each cell had up to five revolutionaries, but they rarely knew who was in the other cells. Secrecy was paramount. Serbia's King Peter was well aware of the Black Hand. His son, Crown Prince Alexander, was an enthusiastic supporter.

How Did the Balkan Wars Change Things?

In the First Balkan War of 1912, Serbia and its neighbors drove the Ottoman Turks back to Istanbul, doubling Serbia's size. The Second Balkan War broke out a year later when Bulgaria made the insane decision to attack Serbia and Greece. The Serbs and Greeks counterattacked Bulgaria's southern border with financial help from France. While the Bulgarians were fighting the Serbs and Greeks, Romania invaded northern Bulgaria. Then, the Ottoman Empire snatched back some of its old territory in Bulgaria. When it lost the war, Bulgaria was a much smaller country, forced to give land to Greece, Romania, and the Ottomans.

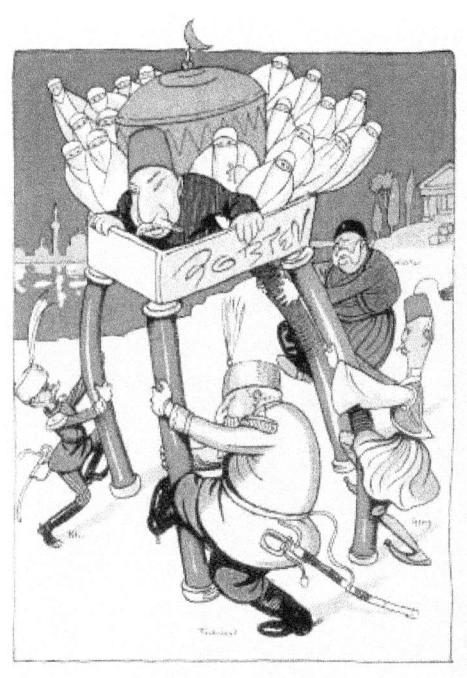

A cartoon of the Balkans attacking the Ottomans in the First Balkan War[6]

Austria-Hungary's military leaders observed the conflict with concern. The Slavs were ambitious people. What if the Southern Slavic people—the Serbs, Bosniaks, Croatians, and Bulgarians—stopped fighting each other? What if they united? They would be a force to reckon with! If Serbia were to lead such a unification, it would be disastrous for Austria-Hungary. It would lose its Balkan provinces and access to the Adriatic Sea. As with Serbia, Austria and Hungary were also landlocked.

A Secret Romance

Austria had once led the German-speaking states in Central Europe, but then Otto von Bismarck burst onto the scene in the mid-1800s. He orchestrated the unification of all the German states except Austria into the German Reich (Empire).

Emperor Franz Joseph of Austria knew he was also in danger of losing Hungary. He struck a deal with Hungary in 1867 to keep that from happening. Instead of simply being part of the empire, Hungary would be an equal partner with Austria. They would be a two-country empire. Each country would have its own parliament and prime minister. Franz Joseph was the head of the military and foreign policy. His only son, Crown Prince Rudolf, would become the next emperor.

The plan soon came crashing down. Rudolf married Princess Stéphanie of Belgium in 1881. At first, they were happy together, but when Stéphanie became pregnant, Rudolf strayed. He became an alcoholic, had many affairs, and picked up venereal disease. He infected his wife with gonorrhea, which left her unable to have more children. She recovered, but Rudolf did not. Their only child was a girl, so he had no male heir. He took morphine to deal with his painful disease and became an addict. Finally, Rudolf and his mistress committed suicide in 1889.

Who would be the next emperor? Franz Joseph's brother, Karl Ludwig, was next in line. However, he died in 1897 from typhoid. Karl's son, Archduke Franz Ferdinand, became the heir to the throne. Yet Franz Ferdinand had a problem. He was in love with the wrong woman. At least, that's what his uncle, Franz Joseph, thought. Austria had stringent rules about who a future king could marry.

Franz Ferdinand was in love with Sophie Chotek. She was a lady-in-waiting, a personal assistant to the wife of the army commander. Sophie's family was not royal. When Franz Joseph discovered Franz Ferdinand was secretly visiting Sophie, he was livid. "She's completely unsuitable!" he raged. "She can't be your wife and the mother of your children. You must marry a royal woman."

Sophie got fired from her post, but Franz had eyes for only her. He refused to marry any of the eligible young ladies of royal blood. Six years passed, and Franz Joseph became desperate as Franz Ferdinand continued to dig in his heels. The emperor was seventy years old. What if he died before the matter was settled? Franz Joseph's sister-in-law convinced him to let Franz Ferdinand marry Sophie.

Sophie Chotek [7]

"You can marry her," the emperor told Franz. "But it must be a *morganatic* marriage. She will not be the empress when you become emperor. Your children will not be royal. None of your children or grandchildren can rule Austria."

Franz Ferdinand married his beloved Sophie on July 1, 1900. Franz Joseph did not attend the wedding. Only Franz Ferdinand's stepmother and two stepsisters celebrated their marriage ceremony. But the happy couple didn't care. After six long years, they were finally together! Little did they know that two bullets would end their lives and begin World War I.

Note to reader: If you are reading an e-book, you can print out the following roundup activity (and others in the book).

On the page with the activity, click "print."

Another way is to take a screenshot by pressing the "Print Screen" (PrtSc) key, which copies the page to your clipboard. You should be able to print from the clipboard. Otherwise, save it to your computer and then print it.

If you are using a Kindle Fire tablet, select "print," choose your printer, and tap "print."

Roundup Activity: Short Answer

Can you answer the following questions in a complete sentence? If you don't remember, review the chapter to find the answer.

1. What countries were in the Triple Alliance and Triple Entente before WWI?
    a. Triple Alliance:
    b. Triple Entente:

2. Why did Britain consider Germany its number one threat before WWI?

3. What new battleship did Britain add in its arms race with Germany? What did Germany focus on in its navy?

4. What was Europe's most unstable region before WWI?

5. What was the Black Hand?

6. Why did Emperor Franz Joseph of Austria strike a deal with Hungary in 1867 to form a two-state empire?

7. Why did Franz Joseph consider Sophie Chotek an unsuitable wife for his nephew, Franz Ferdinand?

Chapter 2: An Assassination in Sarajevo

Franz and Sophie had a baby girl one year after their wedding. Franz named her Sophie after her mother. Two boys completed their family. After fourteen years of marriage, Sophie and Franz were still in love. When it was just their little family, they were happy. Although he was stiff and proper with most people, Franz relaxed around his family. He loved getting down on the floor and playing with his children.

Franz would be the next emperor when his uncle died. Yet, Franz Joseph and the rest of the court went out of their way to make Sophie miserable. She was still a nobody as far as the royal court was concerned. Sophie couldn't sit with her husband at state dinners or ride next to him in royal processions. She couldn't sit in the royal box at the opera. At court balls, Sophie was forced into a corner with the non-royal women.

Archduke Franz Ferdinand and his daughter Sophie [8]

Why Did Franz and Sophie Visit Sarajevo?

One of Franz's roles as archduke was inspector general of Austria-Hungary's armed forces. The empire had soldiers stationed in Bosnia, so Franz traveled there in June 1914 to observe their military exercises. Franz brought Sophie along. It was their fourteenth wedding anniversary, and he wanted to spend it with her away from court. They stayed at a spa resort near Bosnia's capital of Sarajevo. The couple enjoyed escaping the snobbish atmosphere in Vienna. Franz broke the rules and had Sophie sit with him in the open-top car. They were a long way from Vienna, and folks in Bosnia didn't know or care about their morganatic marriage.

Who Was Gavrilo Princip?

Gavrilo Princip was the teenage mastermind of the assassination. He had grown up in poverty in a Serbian family in Bosnia. When Princip was seventeen, he joined Young Bosnia, a secret organization of students (mostly Serbs) in Bosnia committed to revolution. They dreamed of uniting all the Slavic people in Southeastern Europe and had a loose connection to the Black Hand in Serbia. A year earlier, Princip had tried to join the Serbian army to fight the Ottoman Empire, but they said he was too small and weak.

Princip got expelled from school for protesting Austria-Hungary's rule over Bosnia, so he moved to Serbia to attend high school there. A friend showed Princip a newspaper article announcing that Archduke Franz Ferdinand would visit Bosnia that summer. Princip convinced two classmates to join him in an assassination plot against the archduke. All three teens had tuberculosis.

Three assassins—Grabež, Ciganović, and Princip—in May 1914 °

Why and How Did the Black Hand Help with the Assassination Plot?

As we said earlier, the Black Hand wanted to take Bosnia back from Austria-Hungary. The teenage assassins reached out to members of the Black Hand, and they joined the plot. They wanted to provoke Austria-Hungary. If Austria-Hungary declared war on Serbia, the Serbs expected their old ally, Russia, to jump in to defend them. With Russia's help, they thought they could drive Austria-Hungary out of Bosnia and reclaim it for themselves. The Black Hand never dreamed that their actions would ignite a global war.

The Black Hand outfitted the teens with pistols and bombs and taught them how to use them. Princip was the best shot among the three. Meanwhile, Princip wrote to his former schoolmate in Bosnia, Danilo Ilić, asking him to recruit more assassins. Ilić supplied three more teens. Under Bosnian law, teenagers could not get the death penalty. The maximum sentence, even for premeditated murder, was twenty years.

Two of the three boys Ilić recruited had tuberculosis, meaning five of the six assassins had the disease.

Tuberculosis was the leading cause of death in Eastern Europe at that time. Antibiotics had not yet been discovered. Most people survived if they could afford to go to a sanitorium, a medical treatment facility that provided rest, fresh air, and healthy food. For instance, Archduke Ferdinand had tuberculosis as a youth yet survived. However, not everyone could afford good treatment. Living in squalor with little healthy food, the teen assassins faced a high probability of a slow, miserable death. They could not fight in the coming war but could help start it.

The Black Hand smuggled the assassins into Bosnia with bombs and pistols. They gave each teen a vial of cyanide, telling them to swallow the poison as soon as the archduke was dead. This had not been Princip's plan, but the leaders of the Black Hand did not want the murder traced back to them, as they were high-ranking officers in the Serbian army. The teenagers shrugged. If they weren't killed in the assassination attempt, they faced a death sentence from tuberculosis, especially if they were in prison.

Serbia's prime minister, Nikola Pašić, got wind of the assassination plot. He did not want Serbia to go through another war; the country was exhausted and financially crushed by the last wars. They could not withstand an attack by Austria-Hungary. Pašić ordered his military to stop the teens from crossing into Bosnia. "Too late. They're already there," came the answer.

Pašić messaged his ambassador in Austria: "Warn the archduke!" The ambassador reached out to Austria's minister of finance (of all people), vaguely suggesting that "some young Serb might shoot someone." He didn't tell the right people that there was a plot and that they knew the names of the would-be assassins.

How Did Events Unfold on That Fateful Day?

Franz and Sophia awakened to a sunny summer morning on June 28, 1914. It was Sunday, and they attended mass at a chapel in their lodgings. They then sent a telegram to their children. "Momma and Poppa are well. We're looking forward to getting home on Tuesday."

Sophie and Archduke Ferdinand shortly before the assassination [10]

Franz and Sophie got into an open car to drive to the town hall. They treasured this moment of riding together. People lined the street to see the royal couple. Sophie wore a stylish hat with a plume. Netting covered her beaming face, and she held a bouquet of flowers. One of Princip's accomplices from Serbia, Vaso Čubrilović, stood waiting on the sidewalk on the planned route.

Suddenly, the couple's driver saw, out of the corner of his eye, a dark object flying their way. He accelerated to avoid it. Franz also saw it and knocked it away. "It's a grenade!" someone yelled. It bounced off the back of their car, fell to the pavement, rolled under the car behind them, and exploded. A piece of shrapnel grazed Sophie's neck, leaving a trickle of blood. Their driver sped off, but the explosion injured twenty people on the sidewalk and in the car behind them.

Čubrilović swallowed his cyanide pill and jumped into the nearby river. His suicide attempt failed. The river was less than a foot deep, and the cyanide pill was old. It made him vomit but did not kill him. The police dragged him off as an enraged crowd pummeled him. Archduke Ferdinand's car sped to the town hall, unknowingly passing three more assassins. The teens froze, doing nothing. The vehicle was traveling fast, and one later admitted to losing his nerve.

At the town hall, the mayor officially welcomed them to Bosnia, saying everyone was overjoyed at their visit. This was absurd, given that they'd just escaped a bomb attack.

Archduke Ferdinand gave a prepared speech and then changed his itinerary. "Take me to the hospital!" he said. "I want to visit the victims of the bomb attack. Sophie, you stay here. It's too dangerous."

Sophie refused. "I'm going too! My place is with you."

Archduke Ferdinand's chamberlain protested. "It's too dangerous! We should stay here until the troops can be called out to line the roadway."

Military Governor Oskar Potiorek retorted, "The soldiers have been practicing maneuvers. They won't have their dress uniforms if we bring them straight here. The man who threw the grenade was probably acting on his own. Do you think Sarajevo is full of assassins?"

They got back in the car with Potiorek in front. "I'm sure there will be no more trouble," he joked. "These Serb fanatics aren't capable of more than one assassination attempt a day."

However, Potiorek forgot to tell the driver about the change in plans. Instead of driving to the hospital, their driver followed the route they had initially planned. Suddenly, Potiorek realized the mistake. "Turn around!" he shouted at the driver. "You're going the wrong way!"

The driver slammed on the brakes, stalling the car precisely where Gavrilo Princip stood waiting on the sidewalk. Princip stepped up to the car, aimed his pistol, and fired two shots. Potiorek whipped around and saw that the royal couple were seemingly unharmed. Breathing a sigh of relief, he screamed at the driver, "Turn around! Get out of here!"

Potiorek looked back again and was horrified to see blood spurting from Ferdinand's mouth. Sophie saw it, too. "For heaven's sake, what happened to you?" she cried. Then she collapsed into her husband's lap as blood seeped from her lower abdomen.

"Sophie dear! Don't die! Stay alive for our children."

As his attendants tried to assess his wound, the archduke assured them weakly, "It's nothing. It's nothing."

Meanwhile, Princip tried to shoot himself, but the crowd knocked his pistol out of his hand. He swallowed his cyanide pill, yet, as with Čubrilović, it only made him vomit. Later, at his trial, he insisted, "I didn't mean to shoot her! I was aiming for the military governor."

That might have been true. The bullet passed through the car's door before striking an artery in Sophie's groin. She bled out and died as the car sped to the governor's home. Ferdinand had been shot in the neck and died minutes later.

What Happened to the Assassins?

All six teenagers were eventually rounded up, along with Ilić and other adult accomplices. Grabež, Ciganović, and Princip—the three who came from Serbia—were all sentenced to twenty years in prison. All three died in prison from tuberculosis in less than four years. The other three teens received sentences ranging from ten to sixteen years. They were released four years later when the war ended. Most of the adults who were captured were executed by hanging.

Emperor Franz Joseph [11]

How Did the Assassination Impact European Politics and Alliances?

When Emperor Franz Joseph received the news, he remarked, "A higher power has re-established the order which I, alas, could not preserve."[i]

Germany's Kaiser Wilhelm II was on vacation in Norway and grieved over the death of his close friends. Russia's Tsar Nicholas I declared three weeks of mourning. Britain, France, and the United States barely noticed. The Balkans were far away, and assassination attempts were commonplace around the world. However, President Woodrow Wilson's emissary, Edward House, sailed to Europe to assess the situation. He returned and advised President Wilson what he had observed: "It is militarism run stark mad ... there is someday to be an awful cataclysm."[ii]

Bosnia was in an uproar. The Serbs were a minority there. The Catholic and Muslim Bosnians marched through the streets holding black-draped images of Archduke Ferdinand and Sophie. Some attacked Serb neighborhoods, vandalizing Serbian newspaper offices, schools, and the home of the Serbian Orthodox priest.

In Serbia, people danced in the streets. Serbian newspapers launched a disinformation campaign: "Ten thousand Serbs in Bosnia have been hurt or killed!"

Franz and Sophie were quietly buried at their estate in the country. Their children were sent to live with family friends in Switzerland. Two decades later, during World War II, Hitler's Nazi army arrested the two sons and sent them to the Dachau concentration camp. At least 40,000 Jews and political prisoners at Dachau were executed or died from starvation or disease, yet Franz's sons survived the horror.

---

[i] G. J. Meyer, *A World Undone: The Story of the Great War*, 1914 to 1918 (Bantam Dell, 2007). 9.

[ii] Meyer, *A World Undone*, 10.

To War or Not to War?

The Austro-Hungarian leadership met to discuss what to do. Emperor Franz Joseph seemed almost fatalistic about his nephew's death. He had ruled for sixty-six years, one of history's longest-reigning monarchs. He was eighty-four now and not enthusiastic about a war against Serbia. Neither was Hungary's prime minister, István Tisza.

Franz Conrad and Austro-Hungarian troops [12]

However, Franz Joseph's chief of staff, Franz Conrad, had been pushing for war against Serbia even before the assassination. Austria's foreign minister, Leopold von Berchtold, uncharacteristically agreed with Conrad. Ordinarily, Berchtold was passive, yet within two days of the archduke's assassination, he insisted on "a final and fundamental reckoning with Serbia."[i]

Conrad vigorously nodded. "We must take strong action against Serbia. If we don't, these Russian-backed troublemakers will undo us. Germany's got our backs on this one!"

Germany needed Austria-Hungary's support and vice-versa. Yet, any action against Serbia would trigger a reaction from Russia. Neither Austria nor Hungary wanted to fight Russia. Moreover, Austria could not

---

[i] Meyer, *A World Undone*, 20.

go to war without Hungary's consent, and Hungary did not want war. Another issue was that it was summer, and most of the empire's army had been sent home to their villages to help with the harvest.

They had another concern. In three weeks, the French president, Raymond Poincaré, was planning a state visit to Tsar Nicholas II of Russia. If Austria declared war on Serbia before the visit, Poincaré and the tsar could hash out their action plan in person. (At this point, transcontinental phone calls had not been developed, so the French president couldn't pick up a phone and call the Russian tsar.) Emperor Franz Joseph and his war council decided to wait until after Poincaré visited Russia. They would declare war then—*if* it came to that. By mid-August, the harvest would be over, and they could mobilize their troops.

What Ultimatum Did Austria-Hungary Issue to Serbia?

Hungary's Prime Minister Tisza tried to stop, or at least slow, the steady march toward war. Tisza argued for giving Serbia a list of demands, and the Austrian leadership agreed. Tisza wanted the demands to be strict but something that Serbia could accept. He wanted to cure the problem with diplomacy.

"What good would that do?" the Austrian war minister scoffed. "They would interpret it as weakness!"

Everyone else wanted demands that would be impossible for Serbia to accept. That would give them an excuse to invade Serbia when it refused their demands. The question was, what would happen to Serbia if they invaded? Tisza recommended, "We should reduce the size of Serbia, but not annihilate it. If we do that, Russia will most likely accept it and not interfere. However, if we try to obliterate Serbia, Russia will fight to the death."

His idea sounded reasonable. The council agreed to distribute the broken-off parts of Serbia to Albania, Bulgaria, and Greece. That way, the world couldn't accuse Austria-Hungary of going to war just to steal territory. The Austria-Hungary council agreed to send the ultimatum to Serbia.

Austrian Foreign Minister Leopold Berchtold [18]

The next day, Prime Minister Tisza had second thoughts. "If we attack Serbia, I fear Russia will get involved, and we'll end up in a world war," he warned.

The Austrians ignored his concerns. Foreign Minister Berchtold was busy writing the list of demands they would give Serbia.

Tisza looked at the first draft. "I don't really like that word 'ultimatum,'" he said.

"Fine!" said Berchtold, cheerily. "I'll say it's a 'note with a time limit.' We'll give them forty-eight hours to respond."

"What if they don't respond or we don't like their response? What does the letter say we will do?"

Berchtold winked. "We leave them guessing!"

Austria-Hungary's council met again on July 19 to review the final draft. Most of the ten demands were reasonable. Yet, there was one demand everyone felt sure Serbia would reject: Austria-Hungary had to be involved in the assassination investigation.

How Did Escalating Tensions Trigger a Declaration of War?

At 6 p.m. on Thursday, July 23, the day after President Poincaré left Russia to sail back to France, Austria's ambassador delivered the list of demands to Serbia's foreign minister with a warning: "Take it to Prime Minister Pašić. Nothing but full acceptance of all demands will do! He's got until 6 p.m. on Saturday to respond!"

Over the next two days, Britain's newspapers described the demands as "reasonable." A scandalous murder distracted France, and most of its people ignored Serbian affairs. Germany's Wilhelm was off sailing and didn't hear about it. However, Russia's foreign minister, Sergei Sazonov, was seething. "How can Russia stand by while Serbia is humiliated?" he said. "I don't believe for one second that they sent these demands without Germany knowing about it. It's a plot! They want to drive Russia out of the Balkans! They're setting fire to Europe!"

On Friday, twenty-four hours before the deadline, Sazonov ordered the Russian army, "Get ready to mobilize!"

Serbia responded at 6 p.m. on Saturday, July 25: "We're agreeing unconditionally to half the demands. We need clarification on four of the others. However, the one about Austria-Hungary being involved in our investigation of the assassination is a 'no.'"

Serbia's Prime Minister Pašić was not about to let an investigation reveal he knew of the assassination plot in advance. Nor did the high-ranking Black Hand members want to be found out.

Serbia had already started mobilizing its army. Russia held back but growled dire warnings. Serbia and Russia assumed Austria-Hungary would attack at any minute, but it was still mobilizing its troops.

Germany was suddenly concerned. What if Russia attacked its eastern border?

Austria-Hungary depended on France to hold its ally Russia back. That was problematic because France's president was at sea and couldn't be reached. Britain tried to negotiate between Russia and Austria-Hungary, realizing that if France got sucked into war, Britain would inevitably follow. Wilhelm II's younger brother was at the yacht races in Britain with his first cousin, King George V. He messaged Wilhelm, "Georgie wants to stay neutral."

On Monday, July 27, Austria-Hungary's council held a secret vote and declared war on Serbia. Weirdly, they were still two weeks out from fully mobilizing, yet there was no turning back. Two bullets ended a two-decade love story and ignited a global war that raged for four years.

Roundup Activity: Review Questions

1) Who was Archduke Franz Ferdinand, and why was he visiting Sarajevo in 1914?

___

___

___

2) Why did the archduke bring his wife Sophie with him?

___

___

___

3) What did five of the six teenage assassins have in common?

___

___

___

4) Who trained and equipped the teen assassins? Why did the older men get involved?

___

___

___

5) What demand from Austria-Hungary did Serbia refuse to follow? Why?

___

___

___

Chapter 3: Life in the Trenches

Technically, only two nations were at war: Austria-Hungary and Serbia. That didn't last long. Austria-Hungary expected Russia would jump in to defend Serbia but desperately hoped France would convince Russia to hold back. Yet, shortly, all of Europe was set on fire.

Austria-Hungary mobilized most of its army in the south, near Serbia. Russia was already mustering over one million troops. This worried Germany, as it shared a border with Russia. Germany's Kaiser Wilhelm II suggested to Austria, "Invade Serbia's capital, Belgrade, and stop there!" The Serbs had already pulled their army out of Belgrade and were holed up in the interior. Austria-Hungary could take Belgrade without a battle. "My 'Stop-in-Belgrade' proposal would give you a position of strength to negotiate with the Serbs," he advised Emperor Franz Joseph.

Within forty-eight hours after Austria-Hungary declared war on Serbia, Russia had fully mobilized its armed forces, even calling up four million reserves. This ended any hopes of a "Stop-in-Belgrade."

The Siberian mystic, Grigori Rasputin, wrote the tsar, warning, "With war will come the end of Russia and yourselves. You will lose to the last man."

Germany had an old score to settle with France and used this excuse to invade. Germany tried to reassure Britain. "Stay neutral. Even if we invade France and Belgium, we'll restore their borders when all is said and done." The Brits did not find this reassuring. "Wait, Belgium? It's neutral!"

Five weeks after Franz Ferdinand's murder, Germany declared war on Russia. "We have no choice! Russia is mobilizing troops on our border." Britain said it would remain neutral if Germany respected Belgium's neutrality. Germany gave no promises.

The cover of Le Petit depicting the murder [14]

While these negotiations were dragging out, a sensational murder trial in France distracted Paris. Joseph Caillaux was France's former prime minister. He had skillfully defused an earlier rush to war with Germany. However, the newspaper *Le Figaro* had published a scandalous love letter from Caillaux to his current wife Henriette. It was written a few years earlier when they were married to other people but having an affair. An angry Henriette hid a pistol in her fur muff, went to the newspaper office, and shot the editor. Her trial thrust France into a political uproar just when it was supposed to be making delicate negotiations with Germany. Before the murder, Caillaux was almost certain to be reelected. He hoped to work his magic with Germany again. Now, his wife had ruined everything.

Meanwhile, Jean Jaurès, a socialist politician and editor of the newspaper *L'Humanité*, was actively advocating against France going to war with Germany. He was making headway with France's politicians when a university student shot him in the head, killing him instantly. With Jaurès dead, the French socialists lost their antiwar voice. Three days later, France entered World War I on August 3, 1914.

Germany immediately moved into the small country of Luxembourg, which lay between Germany and France. It only had a tiny army of 117,000 men, so resistance was futile. Germany occupied Luxembourg for the rest of the war, and Luxembourg's people suffered near-starvation conditions. They could no longer import food, and the German soldiers commandeered much of what they grew in the country. Germany also invaded Belgium on August 4, 1914. Like Luxembourg, it had declared itself neutral, but Germany plowed through it on the way to France.

Where Were the First Battles?

The first battle of World War I was the ***Battle of Liege*** in Belgium on August 5, 1914. Liege lay on the Meuse River, near Belgium's border with Germany. Belgium only had 35,000 troops fighting 320,000 German soldiers. Belgium's King Albert led his forces in a valiant defense, but the city fell to Germany after ten days. Hundreds of thousands of German troops poured through Belgium, marching toward France. To squelch Belgian resistance, they committed horrible atrocities, shooting over five thousand unarmed citizens, including priests.

The first battle in the Balkans was the ***Battle of Cer***, which began on August 15, 1914, when Austria-Hungary invaded Serbia. After several days, the Serbians drove the invaders out of Serbia. As the panicked Austro-Hungarians fled, many drowned in the Drina River. Serbia scored the first victory, with Austria-Hungary losing twice as many men.

The ***First Battle of the Marne*** in France, which began September 6, 1914, marked a turning point in the war. The Germans had crossed the Belgian border into France and were marching on Paris, confident they could win the war in forty days. They were only thirty miles from Paris with the French army in retreat. Suddenly, the French turned to fight the Germans in the Marne River valley of northeastern France. General

Joseph-Simon Gallieni, the military governor of Paris, launched a counterattack led by General Manoury's Sixth Army and assisted by the British Expeditionary Force.

The French forces attacked Germany's First Army, cutting them off from the other German forces. Meanwhile, the French General d'Esperey's Fifth Army launched a surprise attack on Germany's Second Army. The fighting raged for three days as taxi cabs raced six thousand reinforcements from Paris. The Germans began retreating on September 9 as the French and English pushed them fifty miles north toward the Aisne River. At this point, the German First and Second armies dug in, literally. This was the beginning of *trench warfare* on the *Western Front* (the name for battles fought west of Germany).

What Was Trench Warfare?

The trenches were long ditches dug into the ground. They were about six feet deep and four feet wide. Eventually, the trenches stretched almost five hundred miles, paralleling France's border with Belgium, Luxembourg, and Germany. They reached from the Swiss Alps to the North Sea. Both sides dug trenches for protection while fighting each other.

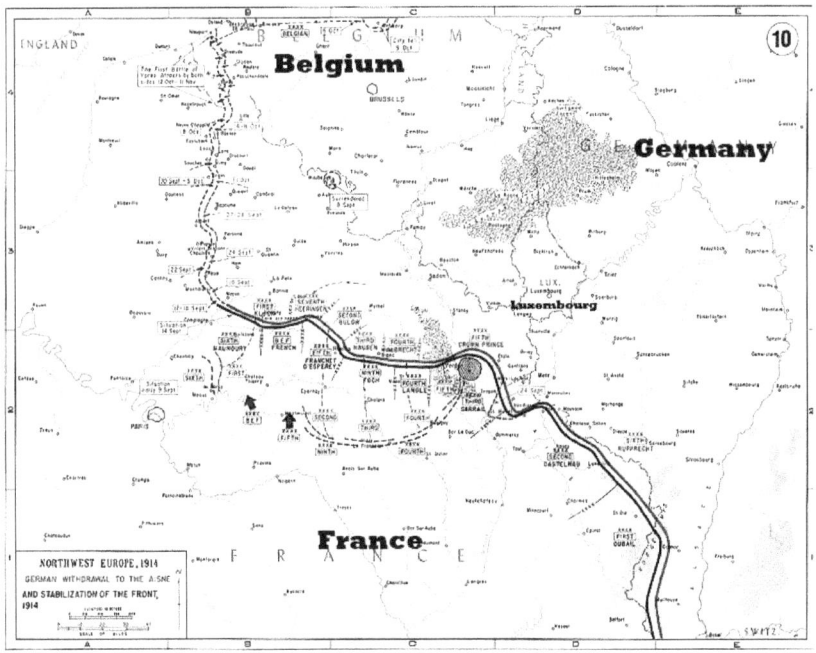

1914 Western Front of trenches near France's border.[15]

The trenches had a "fire step"—a ledge about eighteen inches high—on which the soldiers would stand. From there, they could see and shoot rifles and machine guns at any visible enemies. They also had mortar pits. A **mortar** was something like a cannon. Instead of shooting cannonballs, it launched explosive shells that detonated on impact. Some of the mortar fire had shrapnel, sharp metal fragments that flew through the air at impact. Later in the war, the mortars shot poison gas shells or inflammatory shells that burst into flames. Instead of being launched horizontally, like a canon, they were pointed up. The soldiers shot the mortars at a high, forty-five-degree angle toward the enemy without a specific target.

The trenches gave the soldiers good protection from bullets except when their heads were exposed while shooting. They wore camouflage helmets and covered their machine guns with bushes and netting to disguise them. The trenches also gave some protection from mortar fire unless a shell fell directly into a trench. In that case, it would kill or maim the men in that part of the trench. The soldiers built the trenches in a zig-zag pattern to help protect from mortar explosions. This also ensured that, if the enemy crossed over to their side and jumped into the trench, they couldn't shoot down the corridor and kill all the soldiers in the trench.

The floors of most trenches were dirt, and snow and rain quickly turned it into mud. The soldiers had to stand in the mud and sleep in it at night. Since their feet were continuously wet, they developed "trench foot": numbness, swelling, blisters, and sores. Some soldiers were fortunate enough to have a plank subfloor. The trenches had corridors dug to other trenches further back. It was like a giant maze reaching back to where the latrines (bathrooms) were and where medics cared for the wounded in makeshift field hospitals. Officers also had their command posts in trenches at the rear.

In the damp, unhealthy conditions, soldiers in the trenches suffered horrible diarrhea from diseases like cholera, typhoid fever, and dysentery. They battled lice and a constant onslaught of disease-carrying rats. Soldiers only stayed on the front lines for a few days each month. After duty, they could go to the back trenches for a proper bath, hot meals, and a full night's sleep.

What Was "No Man's Land?"

"No man's land" was the desolate open land in the middle of the battlefield between the French and German trenches. Occasionally, troops from one side would jump out of their trenches and rush the other side. Of course, it was hazardous because they had no protection. Each side strung barbed wire on their side of no man's land to keep the enemy from getting through.

Soldiers in a trench in Belgium in 1917 [16]

Before launching an attack across no man's land, the generals usually ordered heavy artillery bombardment, firing millions of shells to knock down the barbed wire and wipe out the trenches on the enemy's front line. The shells sometimes collapsed the trenches, burying the soldiers alive. Thousands of men died under hails of machine-gun fire while racing across no man's land. Their bodies lay there, sometimes for weeks, until a truce was called to bury the dead.

The soldiers came out of the trenches and gathered the bodies closest to their side, regardless of whether they had been enemy soldiers. These soldiers were usually buried in mass graves. Both sides attempted to keep records of the dead and where they were buried. They collected their "dog tags"—round metal disks the soldiers wore on a chain or cord around their necks. A soldier's name, rank, company, regiment, and religion were stamped on the dog tag.

How Many Teens Were in the Trenches?

At least a quarter million teen boys served in the British army in World War I. The law said that soldiers had to be nineteen or older; however, boys as young as fourteen fought. The army recruiters got a bounty (a certain amount of money) for each soldier they recruited. If a boy was at least five feet, three inches tall, few recruiters asked to see his birth certificate (and many folks did not have them in those days). One fifteen-year-old recruit wrote to his sister, "Dearest Ivy, stand back. I've got my own rifle and bayonet. The bayonet's about two feet long from hilt to end of point."[i]

Germany required healthy males from seventeen to forty-five to serve in the military in WWI. The *Kinderkorps* ("Children's Corps") were units of the youngest and least experienced teen soldiers. Over two-thirds of the Kinderkorps died from October to November 1914 in the First Battle of Ypres in Belgium.

Several soldiers were even younger. Sidney Lewis was twelve when he fought as a British soldier at the Battle of the Somme in 1916. He was tall for his age and eventually grew to be six foot, two inches." His officers apparently did not realize he was only twelve. His mother found out where he had disappeared to and demanded he be sent home. The youngest soldier of WWI was Momčilo Gavrić, an eight-year-old who fought for Serbia.

Leon Abraham, Jewish-Austrian teenage soldier, WWI [17]

---

[i] "The Teenage Soldiers of World War I," *BBC News*, November 11, 2014, https://www.bbc.com/news/magazine-29934965#:~:text=Technically%20the%20boys%20had%20to,Let's%20take%20him.%22

How Did Soldiers Spend Their Time in the Trenches?

A day in the trenches for British soldiers began at 5 a.m. when it was still dark. The soldiers had to "Stand-to-Arms," or be ready to fight. At 5:30 a.m., the British soldiers in the trenches got their daily 2.5-ounce rum ration. At 7 a.m., they ate their breakfast of bacon and tea. They spent the rest of the morning washing themselves, tidying the trench, and cleaning their weapons. Of course, some men were always stationed with rifles and machine guns pointed at the enemy across no man's land.

The main meal of the day was dinner at noon, and then most of the soldiers went to sleep. They would have to be up during the night. At 5 p.m., they had tea—a light meal—and then worked through the night. Some dug more trenches while others ventured out into no man's land to put up more barbed wire. Some men snuck over no man's land to spy out what was happening on the other side. The soldiers also had to go to the back trenches to get more supplies.

How did soldiers cope with the harsh realities of trench life? They wrote their thoughts and experiences in diaries and letters home. They played cards and other games with their fellow soldiers. They read books (provided by the Red Cross) and magazines. Some magazines were "trench magazines" written by soldiers for soldiers. They were full of wry humor, poetry, satire, and cartoons. The horrors of war in the trenches caused some soldiers to question their faith. Others found comfort in prayer, reading Scripture, and singing hymns.

A soldier in a trench reads a letter from home.[18]

In one letter written by a teenage British soldier, Dick, to his mother, he described "a particularly nasty period." After bombarding the German trenches with artillery, his unit went out of the trenches and into no man's land toward the enemy:

> "What a reception the Huns had in store for us, they simply swept the ground with machine gun fire and shrapnel ... I dug myself in and awaited events. It was horrible suspense, as I seemed to be the only man untouched ... being personally acquainted with each man just made matters worse, in fact, it's all wrong to call them men, as they were mostly mere boys. About early afternoon, I was hailed from the trench as to whether it was possible for me to get back. I replied in the affirmative and decided to run the risk of getting potted on the way. So I commenced crawling on my stomach until about a few yards from the parapet, then made a spring and rushed headlong over the top, nearly spoiling the features of a few who happened to be in the trench and were not expecting me."[i]

What Happened on Christmas Day, 1914?

As Christmas approached in that first year of war, the soldiers on both sides were already weary of life in the trenches. They were tired of dead bodies, relentless cold and rain, and living in the mud. Some were literally losing their minds from the unending bullets and shells.

As evening fell on Christmas Eve, 1914, some British soldiers saw a strange sight at the German trenches about thirty yards away.

"What's that they're putting on top of their parapet? It looks like a Christmas tree!"

"It *is* a Christmas tree! Look, they're even putting candles on it!"

"I wanna shoot it down!"

"Are you daft? Why would you want to shoot a Christmas tree? Let's just look at it and enjoy it!"

"Aww ... look! They've got one over there ... and another one there!"

---

[i] "Letters from the First World War: Part I," The National Archives, accessed March 3, 2025, https://www.nationalarchives.gov.uk/education/resources/letters-first-world-war-1915/trenches-mostly-mere-boys/.

The young soldiers gazed at the German line, almost moved to tears by the candles and trees on this desolate Christmas Eve. And then, they heard singing. The boys recognized the tune:

"Stille Nacht, heilige Nacht

Alles schläft; einsam wacht

Nur das traute hochheilige Paar.

Holder Knabe im lockigen Haar,

Schlaf in himmlischer Ruh!

Schlaf in himmlischer Ruh!

"Oh, man! They're singing 'Silent Night'!"

The British were utterly undone by now. Tears streamed down their faces as they sang back:

Silent night, holy night,

Shepherds quake at the sight.

Glories stream from heaven afar,

Heavenly hosts sing Alleluia;

Christ, the Savior, is born!

Christ, the Savior, is born!

The men shouted greetings at each other.

"Happy Christmas!"

"Frohe Weihnachten!"

The Germans declared a temporary truce. The next day—Christmas Day—they would not shoot at each other. Instead, they would bury their dead, relax, and worship.

The following morning, the soldiers emerged from the trenches and met in no man's land. The Germans and British exchanged cigarettes, chocolate, and shots of rum. Then, out of nowhere, a football (soccer ball) rolled through. A few young soldiers began kicking it around, and soon, a lively game ensued. The Scottish Regiment claimed they won, four to one.

British and German soldiers and officers meet in no man's land on Christmas Day 1914.[19]

The Christmas Truce did not happen everywhere along the lines. But, in the places it did, it gave a welcome relief from the drudgery and horror of war. It helped the young soldiers realize the humanity of the soldiers they were fighting. The officers did not like this. If their soldiers made friends with the enemy, they wouldn't want to shoot them. In the following years of war, efforts for other Christmas truces were quickly smothered.

Roundup Activity: Crossword

WWI: Life in the Trenches

Across

4. a cannon-like weapon that shot explosive shells
5. winners of the August 15, 1914 Battle of Cer
7. mystic advisor to Russia's royal family
10. a neutral country invaded by Germany
11. where WWI's first battle was fought on Aug 5, 1914
12. age of WWI's youngest soldier, a Serbian
13. Serbia's capital

Down

1. Germany's inexperienced teen soldiers
2. a common bowel problem in the trenches
3. what country did German invade first?
6. day in 1914 when both sides declared a truce
8. king of Belgium
9. location of a battle in France that began trench warfare

Chapter 4: The Key Battles of World War I

What were the major battles of Western Europe in World War I from 1914 to 1918? Hundreds of battles played out on multiple fronts, yet several seared into our collective memory. These savage battles raged on the four-hundred-mile Western Front in France and Belgium. Millions of soldiers, ankle-deep in muddy trenches and many suffering from the Spanish flu, fought these battles. At least four million teens and adults died in combat. These battles decided the war's ultimate outcome. They put into play lethal new technology, like tanks and chemical weapons, that defined the horrors of modern warfare.

Stalemates where no one won a clear victory frequently marked the trench warfare on the Western Front. The men were stuck there for months on end, making precious little progress. It was a place of mass slaughter, with deaths that were almost meaningless to the course of the war. Clearly, they weren't meaningless to the men in the trenches and their families back home. Yet, the commanders sacrificed thousands of lives to win a few yards of territory.

First Battle of Ypres (October–November 1914), Belgium

The Battle of Ypres ended the "*Race to the Sea.*" The sea in question was the North Sea. After the First Battle of the Marne, the Germans competed to outflank the British and French troops. Both wanted to get to the North Sea first so they could control the Belgian and French coast. Germany's spectacular loss in the First Battle of the Marne in September 1914 ruined their expectations of a quick and easy win. Now, both sides were fighting from trenches. Winning trench warfare involved a steady supply of food and other necessities.

The German commander, General Erich von Falkenhayn, was eager to control the French seaports of Calais and Dunkirk. If Germany held the ports, they could cut off the supplies and additional troops coming over the North Sea from Britain. French General Joseph Joffre was desperately trying to maintain control of the French coast so supply lines could continue. Northern France was also an industrial center, critical to producing weapons and other necessary supplies for war. If France and Britain could not protect the coast, they would lose the war.

German soldiers in a trench in Ypres, 1914 [20]

Ypres was a city in Belgium, just across the border from Calais and Dunkirk, France. The battle ended the Race to the Sea with a victory for the Allies (France and Britain). Inept command and poor strategy caused both sides to botch things. The Germans thought the French had more troops than they really did and gave up early. Yet, they crushed Britain's **regular army** (highly trained professional army). From this point on, Britain had to rely on newly drafted soldiers who lacked the training and experience of the regular army.

Adolf Hitler was twenty-five and a private in the German army. He later told of his "baptism by fire" in the Battle of Ypres. He wrote of racing over turnip fields until crashing into the Allied forces while hearing singing in the distance. The singers were the "innocents," the teenage Kinderkorps who were massacred by the thousands in the dense fog near Ypres.

Battle of Verdun (February–December 1916), France

This battle was the longest in WWI, lasting almost a full year. It was also among the bloodiest. The French lost over 370,000 men, and the Germans lost 330,000. The British and French goal for 1916 was the "Big Push." They wanted to shove the Germans out of northern France while Russia and Italy stormed the Central Powers on other fronts. Germany's modest goal was to take the French town of Verdun near the border of Luxembourg.

Germany planned to shock the French into submission. In the first eight hours of attack, the Germans fired two million shells. They also used flamethrowers for the first time. The carnage was so awful and demoralizing that it impacted the French soldiers' fighting spirit. They mutinied the following year and refused to fight, feeling there was no end in sight to the meaningless violence. To this day, an estimated ten million unexploded shells, some containing arsenic, lie in the forests and fields around Verdun.

The Germans hoped to provoke a French counterattack. Since they held the easily defendable high ground, the Germans could effortlessly wipe out any forces trying to take Verdun back. They planned to "bleed the French white." But their grandiose plans flopped. Although they suffered horrible casualties, the French used ingenious strategies, like drawing the Germans into a counterattack where the French overcame them. By December, the Germans were on the defensive as the French fired over a million shells in six days and blistered them with fighter aircraft attacks. The French captured over thirteen thousand German troops and won the battle.

Battle of the Somme (July–November 1916), France

An Australian soldier, Private Arthur Thomas, wrote about the awe and horror of this battle:

> "We have reached the pit in the theatre of the great drama, and we are feeling fascinated by the terrific ordeal ahead of us. The sky for miles in a semi-circle around us is ablaze, and the colours of the rainbow from star shells illuminate the heavens, and the earth rocks and trembles from the sickening concussion, nothing less than the average imagination of hell."[i]

British Howitzers, Battle of the Somme [21]

For months, the British and French had planned the attack on the German forces at northern France's River Somme. However, when Germany attacked Verdun, most of the French were diverted there. Nevertheless, the British carried out their planned attack. On the first day, 57,000 British soldiers were injured or killed. It was the worst one-day loss in British history. Some said the battle was "lions led by

---

[i] Nick Lloyd, *The Western Front: A History of the Great War, 1914-1918* (W. W. Norton & Company, 2021), Introduction.

donkeys." The soldiers were brave and fierce, but their inexperienced and inept leaders caused thousands of unnecessary deaths.

Lieutenant Alfred Bundy wrote of his experience when the British soldiers "went over the top" from the trenches into no man's land:

> "The din was deafening, the fumes choking and visibility limited owing to the dust and clouds caused by exploding shells. It was a veritable inferno. I was momentarily expecting to be blown to pieces ... Suddenly ... an appalling rifle and machine gun fire opened against us ... I shouted 'down' but most of those that were still not hit had already taken cover. I dropped in a shell hole ... None of our men was visible but in all directions came pitiful groans and cries of pain."[i]

Despite the catastrophic first day, the battle raged for 141 more agonizing days. The British put thirty-two tanks into play for the first time in September—their new secret weapon. Unfortunately, the tanks were prone to mechanical failures. Seven did not start, so only twenty-five rolled into battle. They were excellent for intimidating the Germans, but most got stuck or broke down. Only nine penetrated the German lines.

In November, the British called off the Battle of the Somme. They had only taken six miles of territory. The months-long battle killed or wounded one-third of the three million soldiers who fought on both sides, making it one of history's deadliest battles.

Battle of Passchendaele (July–November 1917), Belgium

This was the third major battle near Ypres. The British and French had been facing off against the Germans there since 1914. Now, the Germans surrounded them on three sides. Ypres was a muddy mess. On the first day, heavy rain fell. The soldiers could not even see the enemy just yards away. The downpour continued for three weeks, turning the battlefield into mud that was waist-deep in places. It drowned soldiers and horses who fell and couldn't get up. The soldiers built "duckboard" bridges over the top of the muck.

---

[i] "Battle of the Somme," National Army Museum, accessed March 3, 2025, https://www.nam.ac.uk/explore/battle-somme.

Medics slog through deep mud carrying a wounded man on a stretcher. [22]

After several weeks of battle, British General Herbert Plumer switched to a "bite and hold" strategy, taking small bits of territory at a time. The soldiers would dig in to hold the new ground and then bite off some more. Fortunately, the sun came out and dried the rain, making maneuvering easier. Passchendaele Ridge was Plumer's ultimate target.

In October, the rains started again, demoralizing the exhausted soldiers. The French and British finally took Passchendaele Ridge on November 10, 1917. They lost 250,000 men, but the United States joined the war and would soon send reinforcements. The Germans weren't so fortunate. They lost 200,000 men and had no replacements.

Battle of Cambrai
(November–December 1917), France

The Battle of Cambrai, which began in northern France on November 20, 1917, marked a change in World War I's strategies. The British were eager to use their tanks to full advantage. They had been tweaking them to be more mechanically reliable and giving the drivers more practice. This was the first time tanks were used on a large scale. They had used thirty-two tanks at the Sommes; at Cambrai, they deployed 378 "male" and "female" tanks. Female tanks used machine guns as weapons, while "male" tanks used heavier "six-pounder" guns (like cannons) that shot six-pound shells with pointed tips.

A battle usually began after several days of bombing the barbed wire and the enemy's front lines. This time, the British used no bombardments. They gave no clue they were up to something. They planned to use the tanks to smash down the barbed wire and protect the soldiers crossing no man's land. The night before they launched their first attack, they brought in the tanks on rail lines that ran to the front.

At dawn, the tanks rolled over no man's land, crushing the barbed wire. The shock and awe factor worked splendidly as the tanks bore down on the front lines. It was foggy, and the Germans could hear the terrifying sound of the approaching tanks but couldn't see them until they suddenly surged out of the mist a few yards away. The battle's first day was a roaring success for the British. They penetrated the German lines by five miles and took 7,500 prisoners.

Railcars delivered the tanks to the British lines. [28]

Rainy weather prevented the British from exploiting the initial triumph. They could only push one more mile into the German territory. On November 30, the Germans counterattacked and pushed the British back. The battle ended in early December, with only small gains made by the British. However, it was a powerful lesson in the advantages of tanks and how to use them successfully.

Second Battle of the Marne (May–August 1918), France

The United States declared war in 1917, which was not a moment too soon for the British. Russia's Communist revolution had knocked it out of the war. Half of the French army was on strike. Britain was hanging on by a thread, and Germany was on the brink of victory. The Germans were only fifty miles from Paris, but the Marne River and a forest called Belleau Wood stood in the way.

The exhausted British and French soldiers were relieved when the US troops joined them. Yet, their brows wrinkled in concern. These Americans were green! They had no fighting experience. They didn't even bring weapons with them.

The American divisions jumped into combat under French command. Among them were the Marines, who earned a reputation for unrelenting toughness. Legend has it that when combat in the Belleau Wood became overwhelming, the French officer yelled, "Retreat!" An American Marine retorted, "Retreat? Hell, we just got here!"

When German troops marched on the city of Reims, the French used an ingenious strategy. The Germans bombarded what they thought were the French trenches. They discovered they were bombing and unleashing poison gas on empty trenches—decoys! The French and American troops then surrounded and trapped the Germans, catching them in their crossfire. This led to the battle's Phase II counteroffensive by the British, French, and Americans. The Allies' victory turned the tide of the war.

Among the Americans who fought in the Battle of the Marne was Douglas MacArthur, chief of staff of the "Rainbow Division" (so-called because it represented multiple National Guard units). MacArthur later became chief of staff of the United States Army. Another US soldier was "Wild Bill" Donovan, director of the Office of Strategic Services (OSS), which later became the CIA. Former President Theodore Roosevelt's son Quentin, a fighter pilot, died in a dogfight with German biplanes. The German pilots gave him a hero's burial with military honors.

French soldiers guide their comrade with bandaged eyes injured by gas, Battle of the Marne. Photo zoomed in.[24]

Battle of Amiens
(August 8-11, 1918), France

This three-day battle was a surprise attack on the Germans by the French, Americans, and British (including Canadians and Australians, who were part of the British Empire). It launched the **Hundred Days Offensive**, which ultimately ended the war. Australian and Canadian shock troops spearheaded a ferocious attack on the first day that nearly broke through the German lines. A **shock troop** is an elite, highly trained military unit that carries out sudden, aggressive assaults designed to overwhelm the enemy.

On the night before the attack, Australian Gunner J. R. Armitage wrote this in his diary:

> "It was utterly still. Vehicles made no sound on the marshy ground ... The silence played on our nerves a bit. As we got our guns into position you could hear drivers whispering to their horses and men muttering curses under their breath, and still the silence persisted, broken only by the whine of a stray rifle bullet or a long-range shell passing high overhead ... we could feel that hundreds of groups of men were doing the same thing— preparing for the heaviest barrage ever launched."[i]

The shock attack launched at 4:30 in the morning as "all hell broke loose." The ground shook, flames pierced the darkness, and exploding bombs deafened the soldiers. Within three hours, the Canadians and Australians overran the German front lines. The Allies captured almost thirty thousand soldiers and took back over a hundred villages and towns held by the Germans. The German General Erich Ludendorff called it "the black day of the German army."

Before this battle, the Allies assumed the war would go on for another year or two. Amiens changed everything. The beginning of the end was in sight, but at a ghastly cost. On that first day, the Canadians suffered 4,000 casualties, and the Allies had 19,000 casualties over the three days. The Germans lost over 26,000 men.

---

[i] "The Battle of Amiens: 8 August 1918," Australian War Memorial, accessed March 3, 2025, https://www.awm.gov.au/visit/exhibitions/1918/battles/amiens.

Meuse-Argonne
(September–November 1918), France

The Meuse-Argonne Offensive was the battle that ended the war. It was the largest battle in United States military history, with 1.2 million American soldiers. It was also the deadliest battle in American history, killing over 26,000 US military men. The Germans also lost 28,000 of their 450,000 men. About 800,000 French troops fought alongside the Americans, and 35,000 died. Another interesting contribution was 850 fighters from Siam (Thailand). After America entered the war, Siam and multiple other countries followed. Siam even added the color blue to its flag to match the red, white, and blue colors of the British, French, United States, and Russian flags.

American machine guns shot down this German biplane in the Argonne.[25]

The battle raged in northern France's Argonne Forest and along the Meuse River. An influenza epidemic called the *Spanish flu* was encircling the globe. It killed fifty million people, including 45,000 American soldiers. The soldiers in the trenches fought the flu while fighting the enemy. Over 1,400 American soldiers died from the Spanish flu in October 1918.

The Meuse-Argonne Offensive had three phases. The first began on September 26. Captain Harry S. Truman, who later became an American president, led one of the artillery groups. In three hours, the American military spent about one million dollars a minute on ammunition. The inexperienced American forces made no gains against the Germans, and the German counterattacks even took new land. However, the French made some headway.

Phase two began on October 4. Brigadier General Douglas MacArthur's men discovered a poorly defended gap in the German Hindenburg Line at Côte de Châtillon. The Americans broke through the German line in the Argonne Forest, taking ten miles of territory. This was the breakthrough that ultimately won the battle. The French took twenty miles, reaching the Aisne River.

In phase three, the Americans gained fifteen miles, and the French captured twice as much. They took control of the entire Argonne Forest. The Americans held off the German forces while the French crossed the Aisne River, stormed the town of Le Chesne, and took control of the railroad hub. The Germans called an ***armistice*** (an agreement to stop fighting), which ended the war. At 11:00 a.m. on November 11 (the eleventh hour, day, and month), Germany and the Allies signed the armistice, ending World War I.

Roundup Activity: Don't forget the date!

Match each date with the correct battle. Check your answers in the back of the book.

October–November 1914   Battle of Amiens

February–December 1916   Battle of Cambrai

July–November 1916   Battle of Passchendaele

July–November 1917   Battle of the Somme

November–December 1917   Battle of Verdun

August 8-11, 1918   First Battle of Ypres

September–November 1918   Meuse-Argonne Offensive

Chapter 5: The Forgotten Fronts

Most movies and books about World War I focus on the Western Front—the battles in France and Belgium. Yet, there was far more to the story. World War I also had an Eastern Front, twice as long as the Western Front. It reached from the Black Sea to the Baltic Sea and mainly involved Russia's struggles against the Central Powers of Austria-Hungary and Germany.

World War I also had an Italian Front. When the war began, Italy was a member of the Triple Alliance with Germany and Austria-Hungary. However, Italy initially wanted to stay out of the war. In 1915, Italy switched to the other side, joining Britain, France, and Russia.

The war began in the Balkans, and the Balkan Front swirled around the Serbians' struggle against Austria-Hungary, Germany, and Bulgaria. Meanwhile, the Ottoman Empire fought on two fronts in World War I: against Russia in the Caucasus Front between the Black Sea and the Caspian Sea and in the Middle Eastern Front, from Syria to Egypt.

Russia and the Eastern Front

After Austria-Hungary declared war on Serbia, Russia entered the war on Serbia's side. Russia gathered its army on its border with Austria. The Russians hoped Germany would only consider it a local conflict. Germany dashed that hope when it declared war on Russia three days later.

Germany was already planning to attack France. War with Russia would place Germany in an awkward position with enemies on both sides. Thus, Germany developed the "Schlieffen Plan." If it went to war with Russia, the first thing it would do was march through Belgium into France and take Paris. German officials were confident they could do this before Russia could get its army in place. Then, they would be free to concentrate solely on Russia.

That's precisely what the Germans did. They marched through Belgium and were only a few miles out of Paris when the French and British stopped them. The plan fell to pieces when the German army was forced to hunker down in trenches and fight the British and French for years.

While the Germans focused on France, Russia attacked East Prussia, a German kingdom surrounded by Russia on its east and south. Russia had a reputation for doing everything at a snail's pace, yet it surprised Germany with the speed and precision it used to invade East Prussia. On August 17, Russia deployed two armies of 200,000 soldiers to capture East Prussia's capital of Königsberg.

The brilliant German commander, Paul von Hindenburg, rushed to lead East Prussia's defense. He knew something about the two Russian generals leading the attack on East Prussia, Samsonov and von Rennenkampf. They hated each other so much that they refused to speak to each other. They also had a bad habit of using the radio to give battle plans to their troops. The Germans were experts at tapping the Russian radio signals, listening in, and getting one step ahead of them.

The Germans killed 120,000 Russians in several days of merciless bombing. It was a ghastly failure for Samsonov. He shot himself rather than surrender, but his men surrendered anyway the next day, August 30. Hindenburg took 100,000 Russian prisoners of war and forced the rest of Samsonov's army to retreat from Prussia.

"Russian Cold Steel in Prussia" [26]

Hindenburg then marched north to confront von Rennenkampf. The Russians were running out of supplies and had far fewer men than the German army. Hindenburg defeated them on September 16, taking 45,000 more Russian prisoners. The remaining Russians fled Prussia and dared not return for the rest of World War I.

In April 1916, Russia's commanders met to discuss strategy. Tsar Nicholas II attended as Russia's supreme commander. Yet, he had no training or experience in war. The leading generals hashed out the plan while he sat quietly. Everyone was gloomy. The Russians had significantly sacrificed to distract the Germans from the Western Front.

General Alexei Brusilov begged for the chance to attack the Austrians at Russia's Southwestern Front (present-day Ukraine). The other generals said yes but doubted anything would come of it. The **Brusilov Offensive** (June–September 1916) launched at the city of Lutsk. Joseph Ferdinand, the Austrian general, was over-confident. He had 200,000 men to defend against Brusilov's 150,000 men. To everyone's surprise, Brusilov's brutal assault broke through the Austrian lines. He captured 26,000 prisoners on the first day.

Austrian commander Conrad von Hötzendorf hurried back from his failed campaign in Italy. He warned the Germans, "This is the greatest crisis we have yet to face in this war!" The Germans sent four divisions from the Western Front to bail out the Austrians. It came at a painful cost, leaving them vulnerable to the attacks at Verdun and Somme days later.

Meticulously prepared, the "Iron General" Brusilov crushed the Austrian and German armies. He killed or wounded over a million soldiers and took 400,000 prisoners. He snatched more territory than any other Allied offensive in World War I, pushing Austria-Hungary out of the war. However, the Russians also lost over a million men. Things were unraveling back in Russia, and the Brusilov Offensive shut down in late September.

The Italian Front

Although Italy bravely fought the Central Powers, it rarely appears in the spotlight of World War I history. Italy became a united country a half-century before World War I. Before that, it was a collection of states, some of which were colonies of other countries. That's why it seemed weird when Italy joined the Triple Alliance with Germany and Austria-Hungary. Austria once had colonies in Italy and had stood in the way of its independence.

Joining the Triple Alliance had not helped Italy's strained relationship with Austria-Hungary. This was one reason Italy pulled out of the Triple Alliance and joined with Britain, France, and Russia after the war started. Britain also encouraged Italy with enticing promises: "Switching sides is to your advantage! Help us in the war, and you'll get new territory from Austria-Hungary once we defeat it!"

Italy joined the war in 1915 by declaring war on Austria-Hungary (but not Germany). The first battles were in Isonzo, Slovenia, part of Austria-Hungary at that time. Italy's early days in the war were disappointing. Italy had more soldiers, but the Austrians had more experience. They killed a quarter of the Italian army within months. Pope Benedict XV fumed: "We shouldn't have a war between two Catholic countries! It's nothing but a useless massacre." When the Italians heard this, many deserted the army or refused to enlist.

Things continued to go south for Italy. Messy politics distracted Russia, so Austria moved more soldiers from Russia to Italy. When Italy declared war on Germany in 1916, German soldiers headed to Italy. In October 1917, 400,000 men attacked the Italian army at Caporetto, near Italy's border. In the **Battle of Caporetto**, the Germans and Austrians surrounded the Italian army and killed 11,000 men. They also took more than a quarter-million prisoners of war. The battle was among World War I's most disastrous defeats.

Italian soldiers await the enemy.²⁷

Finally, Italy had a breakthrough. It won two decisive battles at the Piave River in northwestern Italy. Austria-Hungary and Germany attacked Italy in the **First Battle of the Piave River** (November 1917). The Italian army was in retreat after the humiliating loss at Caporetto. And then, it happened. "Stop here!" their new chief-of-staff, Armando Diaz, commanded as they entered the mountain pass. "We'll use the steep terrain to our advantage." The Italians blocked the enemy and scored a win at last!

Italy got more welcome news. Austria and Hungary's union was crumbling. The Austrians and Hungarians were starving from a failed crop and dying from the Spanish flu. Some of the ethnic minorities in the empire wanted independence, encouraged by US President Woodrow Wilson. The uneasy relationship between Austria and Hungary subdued their fighting spirit.

The ***Second Battle of the Piave River*** (June 1918) started with another attack by Austria-Hungary. The British and French sent six divisions from the Western Front to help the Italians. Then, the Italians got crucial information: "They're planning to attack on June 15 at 3 a.m."

Italy's commanders chuckled. "All right. We'll start bombing them at 2:30 a.m. They won't dare leave the trenches with shells flying!"

As predicted, many Austro-Hungarians held back, but some brave units crossed the Piave River. However, the Italians launched a counterattack and chased them back to the river. By this time, the Italian bombers had destroyed most of the bridges over the swollen and swift river. The Austro-Hungarians had to choose between being mowed down by Italian bullets on the riverbank or trying to swim across. Many Austro-Hungarians drowned in the river. The Austro-Hungarian forces on the other side retreated, and the Italians won.

The Balkan Front

The two shots that started World War I rang out in the Balkans in Southeastern Europe. What was so important about the Balkans? Weren't they just a group of impoverished countries with an agricultural economy and few natural resources? Yes, but their location was pivotal. They were at a strategic crossroads between Russia, Austria-Hungary, and the Ottoman Empire. The Balkan countries were the gateway from Asia to Europe.

The Balkan region of World War I was called the ***Balkan Theatre.*** As mentioned, Austria-Hungary invaded Serbia in August 1914, beginning the ***Serbian Campaign.*** The Serbians chased the invaders off, yet the Austro-Hungarians tried again and lost. They tried a third time and lost again.

The fourth time, in October 1915, was the game-changer. Serbia had fought a Typhus epidemic early in 1915 that killed thousands and weakened the population. In addition, Austria-Hungary synchronized its attack with Germany and Bulgaria. Austria-Hungary and Germany attacked from the north and Bulgaria from the south. They caught the Serbs between three armies. Britain and France sent four divisions to northern Greece but couldn't get past the Bulgarians to Serbia. The Serbs fought fiercely, but the Germans and Austro-Hungarians kept driving them south. As the Serbian army retreated, women carrying their children and old people riding in carts fled south with them.

In the *Great Retreat*, the Serbs first hoped to sneak into Macedonia. From there, they could link up with the British and French divisions. Instead, they found themselves stuck in Kosovo. The Germans, Austro-Hungarians, and Bulgarians formed an impenetrable wall on three sides. On November 23, 400,000 thousand Serbian soldiers, women, children, and elderly people had only one route of escape. The jagged and aptly named Accursed Mountains (Albanian Alps) lay between them and the sea. The Serbs pulled their aging, nearly blind King Peter in an oxcart as they climbed the mountains, hoping to escape to the Adriatic Sea, where the Allied ships waited.

The Accursed Mountains, where over 200,000 Serbians died in the Great Retreat.[38]

The people in the Great Retreat experienced utter horror in the mile-high, inhospitable mountains. It was the dead of winter, and thousands froze to death. Thousands more starved or died from illness. Meanwhile, the Austrians flew over, dropping bombs. The Serbians' flight to the sea passed through Montenegro, which Austria-Hungary attacked, trying to stop the Serbs. Montenegro's small army fought fiercely for twenty days but finally surrendered. Yet, their courageous battle enabled the Serbs to escape the Austro-Hungarians.

Over half of the 400,000 Serbs died on the trek over the mountains. They finally reached the Adriatic Sea in February 1916. Safety was in sight! The Allied ships evacuated them to Greece, and the remnants of the Serbian military joined the Allied army. They fought at the **Macedonian Front**, which ran from the Adriatic Sea to Bulgaria's border with Greece.

The Serbs took back part of Macedonia from the Bulgarians. In the **Vardar Offensive** of September 1918, after the Austro-Hungarians and Germans withdrew from the Balkans, the Serbians, Greeks, and French defeated Bulgaria. Germany's Kaiser Wilhelm II telegrammed the Bulgarian tsar, Ferdinand I: "Disgraceful! Sixty-two thousand Serbs decided the war!"[1]

The Ottoman Empire and the Caucasus and Middle Eastern Fronts

The Ottoman Empire, led by the Turks, fought on the side of the Central Powers (Germany, Austria-Hungary, and Bulgaria) in World War I. Once the world's largest empire, it was already falling apart before the war. Folks called it "the Sick Man of Europe." The Ottoman Empire lost most of its European territory in the war. After the war, it dissolved as an empire.

When the war first began, the Ottoman Empire was weighing its options and negotiating with both sides. It only took three days for the Ottoman war minister, Enver Pasha, to throw his hat in with Germany. The Germans offered a secret deal. "Come in on our side, and we'll give you two warships, the SMS *Goeben* and the SMS *Breslau*. We'll also give you two million in gold."

The Ottoman capital of Constantinople (Istanbul to the Turks) was located on the Bosphorus Strait between the Black Sea to the Marmara Sea. The Ottomans also controlled the Dardanelles Strait, which connects the Marmara Sea to the Aegean Sea and the Mediterranean

---

[1] "Serbian Campaign," Military Wiki, accessed March 3, 2025, https://military-history.fandom.com/wiki/Serbian_campaign#1915.

Sea. Russia, which borders the Black Sea, sent many ships through the Bosphorus and Dardanelles straits (and still does today).

What Germany really wanted to do was raid Russian ships and ports in the Black Sea. So, they gave the ships to the Ottoman Empire, yet the German crew remained. They just changed their uniforms and ship flags. German Admiral Wilhelm Souchon commanded the ships.

The Dardanelles and Bosphorus Straits [29]

Souchon convinced Enver to let him sail German and Ottoman ships into the Black Sea. They torpedoed a Russian gunboat at the Black Sea port of Odessa. They also opened fire on two other Russian port cities, although they gave the civilians two hours to leave town. Because Russian ships were shadowing the German and Ottoman ships, Souchon insisted they had "opened hostilities." He ignored the fact that the Russian ships never fired on the German and Ottoman ships.

British Admiral Winston Churchill ordered British ships to fire on Ottoman ships. They also bombed Ottoman forts at the Bosphorus Strait. The Ottoman Empire officially declared war on November 11, 1914.

Most Ottomans were Muslim, especially in Turkey and the Middle East. Ottoman Sultan Mehmed V called for a "*Great Jihad*," trying to make the conflict a holy war for Muslims. However, the Middle Eastern Muslims were disinterested.

The Ottoman army fought in the Balkans, the Middle East, and in northwest Asia's Caucasus region. Its ***Caucasus Campaign*** lasted from 1914 to 1918 and targeted Russia's territory near the Black Sea's eastern shores. This land had once belonged to the Ottomans, and they wanted it back. The Germans and Austro-Hungarians nodded approvingly when the Ottomans focused on the Black Sea. It helped keep the Russians distracted from Europe. However, Russia fared better in the Caucasus Front than the Ottoman Empire, with half as many casualties. Ultimately, the campaign ended when Russia's revolution forced it out of the war.

The ***Gallipoli Campaign*** (February 1915–January 1916) took the struggle back to the Dardanelles Strait. As we said, the Ottoman Empire's capital of Istanbul (Constantinople) reigned over the straits leading to the Black Sea. This was problematic for Russia, so the Allies planned to occupy the capital and control the traffic in and out of the Black Sea. The Allies launched the campaign at the Gallipoli Peninsula, which is separated from the mainland of Turkey by the Dardanelles Strait.

In this campaign, the Allies introduced ***amphibious landings*** to modern warfare, where soldiers jumped out of landing craft to storm the beach. The landings worked well, but the campaign was an embarrassing debacle for the Allies. Bad weather battered their ships, and they suffered from poor planning, inexperienced troops, and a lack of equipment and ammunition. The huge Ottoman Empire diverted thousands more men to protect the straits.

On the ***Middle Eastern Front***, the Ottoman Empire fought in the ***Sinai and Palestinian Campaign*** for control of Egypt and Palestine. Egypt was critical because of the Suez Canal. It is the only way for ships to go from the Mediterranean to the Red Sea (and ultimately the Indian Ocean) without having to sail the long and dangerous voyage around the bottom of Africa.

T. E. Lawrence wore Arab clothing while fighting in the Middle East in WWI.[30]

This campaign began when the Ottomans invaded the Sinai Peninsula, where Egypt borders today's Israel and the Gaza Strip. After the Suez Canal was built (1869), the British had occupied Sinai (beginning in 1888) to protect the Suez Canal. The Ottoman Empire had ruled Palestine since 1516. Now, the Ottomans wanted to control the canal. Their attempt to take it was an abject failure. The British chased them out of the Sinai Peninsula. Led by Lawrence of Arabia (Lieutenant-Colonel T. E. Lawrence), the British then proceeded to invade Palestine, capturing Gaza and Jerusalem in 1917.

Roundup Activity: True or False?

Mark each statement with a "T" for true or "F" for false. Check your answers in the back of the book.

( ) 1. The Forgotten Fronts refer to the lesser-known Eastern, Italian, Balkan, Caucasus, and Middle Eastern fronts.
( ) 2. Some of the Forgotten Fronts were in the Middle East and northwestern Asia.
( ) 3. The Battles of Verdun and Somme took place on the Italian Front.
( ) 4. The German's "Schlieffen Plan" involved fighting Russia first and then attacking France.
( ) 5. Russia's Brusilov Offensive captured more territory than any other Allied offensive in World War I.
( ) 6. Italy scored two vital wins in the Battles of the Piave River.
( ) 7. The Great Retreat took the Serbians through the jagged Accursed Mountains.
( ) 8. The Ottoman Empire joined the war when Russian ships fired on Ottoman ships.
( ) 9. The Caucasus Campaign focused on the Black Sea's eastern shores.
( ) 10. The Ottomans' attempt to take the Suez Canal failed and caused them to lose Jerusalem and Gaza to the British.

Chapter 6: The Technology of World War I

The turn of the twentieth century introduced groundbreaking technological breakthroughs. Ordinary people started using the conveniences we take for granted today, like telephones, automobiles, and airplanes. Mind-blowing new technology reshaped how war was done. Terrifying tanks rumbled over battlefields. Fighter planes engaged in dogfights overhead. New weaponry, like grenades, machine guns, and poison gas, made war more deadly than ever.

What Transportation Inventions Changed the Course of the War?

Tanks were secretly developed during WWI by the British, who used their Mark I for the first time in 1916. These tanks had a steering tail in the back, which did not work as well as hoped. The earliest tanks had a few kinks to work out before they could be used significantly. Even so, they had a shock and awe factor that terrified the German soldiers.

By the war's end, Britain had manufactured 2,600 tanks, which rolled over trenches, delivering artillery fire from their protected cabins. France produced about 3,000 tanks during WWI. They invented a fully rotating turret, a structure on which a tank's gun was mounted that provided a protected spot for the gunner. The German army sometimes captured the British and French tanks. They turned them on the enemy and used them as prototypes to learn how to make them. However, the Germans only produced twenty A7V tanks by the war's end.

Airplanes first played a significant role in warfare in World War I. Orville and Wilbur Wright had only invented them eleven years before the war began. These two brothers flew their first successful flight in 1903 at Kitty Hawk on North Carolina's Outer Banks. They started building airplanes for sale in 1909 and taught army officers how to fly. In 1912, they organized the first armed flight, in which they demonstrated how a machine gun could be shot from a plane.

The Wright Brothers' first flight at Kitty Hawk [31]

In 1911, three years before World War I began, the Institute of International Law proposed a law that airplanes could only be used on *reconnaissance* missions (spying out the enemy's position and strength and the area's terrain). They were afraid airplanes would attack undefended cities. Using airplanes for reconnaissance saved the day for the Allies in the first month of the war. It helped them stop the Germans from reaching Paris when they invaded France. British spy planes discovered the German forces were about to surround the British Expeditionary Force. The British army withdrew in time, saving 100,000 soldiers.

In the early days of the war, if British and German reconnaissance planes met in the air, they would smile and wave at each other. Air combat was not yet a thing, but that changed quickly. At first, pilots started lobbing grenades at enemy planes. Some even threw grappling hooks, trying to catch the other airplane and send it into a tailspin. The pilots tried to shoot at each other with pistols or rifles, but it was hard to aim.

On August 23, 1914, a British pilot used a machine gun for the first time to fire on a German plane. After that, most fighter planes carried machine guns. Some had gunners that flew with the pilot. Shooting a machine gun from an aircraft got complicated because the propeller was in the way if the target was directly in front. Engineers experimented with systems to synchronize the rotating propeller with volleys from the gun so the bullets would not hit the propeller blades.

Before the war, a Russian pilot named Pyotr Nesterov first flew an airplane in a loop. This skill came in handy when pilots engaged in "dogfights," or battles in the air. Nesterov was a daredevil, and in September 1914, he tried to sideswipe an Austrian plane. Both airplanes crashed, killing everyone. It was the first time one airplane brought down another.

Anyone familiar with the *Peanuts* comic strip remembers the dog Snoopy perched on his doghouse, wearing a helmet and goggles with a scarf streaming behind him. In his imagination, Snoopy is in a "dogfight" with the Red Baron. The actual Red Baron was Baron Manfred von Richthofen, a German fighter pilot. A pilot with exceptional skills in dogfights was called an "ace." The Red Baron was the "ace of the aces," World War I's best air combat pilot. Richthofen liked to paint his aircraft red (hence the name Red Baron). He shot down eighty enemy planes before a bullet fired by ground antiaircraft killed him while he was flying over the Somme River.

Manfred von Richthofen, the Red Baron [32]

Zeppelins were long, cylinder-shaped, rigid aircraft used by Germany. They used hydrogen gas bags to stay in the air. Unlike balloons, they could be steered with a rudder for horizontal movement. If the pilot wanted to go up or down, he used a sliding weight. A Zeppelin had a 420-foot-long aluminum body, longer than a football field. A propeller made the craft move forward at thirty miles per hour, and it could carry fifty people.

When WWI began, the Germans used Zeppelins to drop bombs. Zeppelins could move stealthily through the sky, especially if it was cloudy or nighttime. Their engines were quiet, and a pilot could cut its engines and let it just float in total silence.

Fifteen-year-old William Gedge recalled his experience in January 1915 when a Zeppelin flew over Great Britain and bombed the Norfolk coast. It was the first time a Zeppelin dropped bombs on civilians:

> "I remember Yarmouth being bombed ... by Zeppelins—we were the first town in England to be bombed by Zeppelins. And I can remember being in the bar with my father, and the whole place shook and he says, 'Open the door boy, there's somebody trying to get into the bar.' And I went to the door, and I didn't see ... if there was a flash, I couldn't see them, the bombs, but I could hear half a dozen bombs falling in a straight line down Southgates Road, which is near the fish wharf right in the other end of the town."[i]

A Zeppelin over a battlefield near Verdun, France, in 1916 [33]

---

[i] "Voices of the First World War: Zeppelins Over Britain," Imperial War Museums, accessed March 3, 2025, https://www.iwm.org.uk/history/voices-of-the-first-world-war-zeppelins-over-britain.

At first, nobody knew what to do when a Zeppelin—"the big silver cigar"—flew over their town to drop bombs. Some fled to nearby fields, which left them more exposed. In London, people escaped to subway stations, where they could be underground. Some mothers took their children to the subway to sleep every night, putting blankets down on the hard floor.

Eventually, British fighter pilots learned how to shoot Zeppelins down with new technology. They used two types of bullets. **Incendiary bullets** caught fire when they struck a hard object. They worked nicely to set the Zeppelin's hydrogen gas bags on fire. **Pomeroy explosive bullets** exploded when they hit the Zeppelin, creating a large hole.

Strategic bombers were airplanes developed in World War I for dropping bombs. The Russians were the first to use four-engine planes called Sikorsky Ilya Muromets to drop bombs in 1914. By 1916, the British introduced the Handley Page Type O bomber, the world's largest airplane at that time. It carried the heaviest bomb of that day, weighing 1,650 pounds. The Type O bombers also carried multiple smaller bombs. By 1917, the Germans used the Gotha, a twin-engine biplane (two pairs of wings, one over the other), for dropping bombs.

Russia dropped bombs on supply depots, railway yards, and enemy troops. England's bombs initially targeted the Zeppelin stations and factories. The Germans had no qualms about dropping bombs on towns and cities, killing civilians. However, Kaiser Wilhelm II forbade his bombers from dropping bombs on London since King George V was his first cousin and close friend. He later lifted the ban after the British started bombing German cities.

Anti-aircraft warfare was developed to fight the new terror of bombs dropping from the sky. In September 1915, the Serbians desperately tried to shoot Allied airplanes dropping bombs on their city of Kragujevac. Their shotguns and machine guns damaged some of the planes but didn't bring them down. However, one soldier fired a Turkish canon at an airplane and successfully knocked it out of the air. The cannon wasn't an official anti-aircraft weapon but an ordinary cannon left over from the 1912 Balkan War.

The British and other armies quickly developed anti-aircraft guns that were larger, heavier versions of the machine guns carried by infantry. The anti-aircraft guns were mounted like cannons on trucks with rotating platforms to aim at passing airplanes. Crews of up to twelve men fired the weapons.

A six-inch anti-aircraft gun in Dover Harbor, England [84]

Like airplanes, *observation balloons* were used in World War I to spy on enemy positions and terrain. They used hydrogen as fuel. They could fly miles high, putting them out of range of anti-aircraft fire. However, if they went too high, the passengers would get "air sickness" unless they had tanks for supplemental oxygen.

"Captive" balloons had a tether or cable attached to a vehicle on the ground with a large spool and winch that could move them up and down. These balloons were sometimes sausage-shaped, like Zeppelins, but fatter and shorter. They had a gondola to ride in. "Untethered," or free balloons were hard to steer, but the Allies used them to drop propaganda leaflets over the German lines. "Surrender! Fighting is futile!" they read. "You're better off as prisoners of war in our camps than you are right now."

Submarines became essential element of World War I, starting with the Germans. In the early days of the war, the German submarines surfaced before they fired, allowing the enemy crew to get off their ship into lifeboats. Later, German submarines began "unrestricted submarine warfare," stalking and firing on merchant ships and passenger ships without warning. They even sank vessels belonging to neutral countries (like America).

German "U-boat" submarines were over two hundred feet long. On the surface, they traveled with diesel engines at about thirteen knots (fifteen miles per hour). They could stay underwater for about two hours using battery power, but their speed was only seven knots (eight miles per hour).

The Allies began using submarines in 1915, starting with the British E-class submarines they had built before the war. They were smaller and faster than the German submarines.

German U-boat UB 14 with its crew, 1918 [85]

Trench railways carried food, ammunition, and supplies to the millions of men entrenched on the front lines. They also transported the wounded to hospitals, although doctors at the front could provide immediate aid. As mentioned, the Allies even brought tanks to the trenches by rail.

Before the war, the French had already developed portable, prefabricated track systems. Soldiers could quickly lay the tracks over all types of terrain. The Allies often used horses to pull the trains in the daytime because the puffs of steam from locomotive engines could give away their position. They employed so many horses in battles and for transportation that feed for the horses was Britain's largest export to France in WWI. The Allies had almost a thousand steam locomotives running the rails at night. The Germans also used prefabricated tracks and produced two thousand locomotives during the war.

What New Weapons Were Used in World War I?

Chemical weapons were banned by the Hague Convention of 1899 with the agreement of twenty-seven nations, including Austria-Hungary, Britain, France, Germany, and Russia. Nevertheless, poison gas became a horrifying reality of World War I. In the first month of the war, the French began throwing small grenades holding tear gas into the German trenches. The gas pooled in the trenches, causing eye and skin irritation, coughing, and vomiting. The idea was to drive the Germans out of the trenches, yet the grenades weren't especially effective.

In 1915, the Germans released clouds of chlorine gas on British and Canadian soldiers in the Second Battle of Ypres. They lined up cylinders of the liquid gas on their front lines, waited until the wind blew toward the Allies, and then opened the cylinders. The Canadians and British who got concentrated fumes went blind, and some choked to death. The gas killed or injured at least six thousand soldiers.

The devastating new weapon of war demanded protection. Just before the war, a brilliant African American named Garrett Morgan invented a precursor to the gas mask. It was a "smoke protection hood," meant to protect from smoke inhalation. The US Navy gave Morgan a contract to produce the hoods to protect soldiers. The filtering material in the mask gave some protection from chlorine and mustard gas.

The British developed a carbon monoxide respirator because unexploded shells landing in or near the trenches gave off carbon monoxide. The Germans took the respirator a step further by putting gas-neutralizing chemicals in the respirator's air filters.

A German soldier wearing a gas mask, WWI. [36]

Trench guns (combat shotguns) were shotguns with shortened barrels that made them easier to use in the trenches. Before WWI, most shotguns were single shot, but they were adapted to fire multiple rounds without reloading. The soldiers also had bayonets (something like a long dagger) attached to their guns for one-to-one combat. The bayonets were handy when the soldiers needed to open a can, toast bread, or scrape mud off their boots.

Bolt-action rifles were the most common guns in WWI. These rifles could be reloaded five times faster than muzzle-loading guns. More importantly, the soldiers didn't have to stand up to reload, which was helpful while dodging enemy fire. Just as you would open and close a bolt on a door, a soldier reloaded his gun by lifting the handle and pulling it back to eject the used shells. He inserted new shells, pushed the handle forward to reload, and then pushed the handle down to lock it.

Bolt-action rifles were adapted to hold more rounds so the soldiers didn't have to stop and reload as much. They also had improved sights so the soldiers could aim better. The soldiers' constant challenge was keeping their guns dry and clean, so improved mechanisms enabled reliable operations even in bad weather. Like shotguns, the rifles could fire multiple rounds and had bayonets.

Machine guns were invented in 1885 by British inventor Hiram Maxim. Ten years later, the Americans took it to the next level by using gas pressure from an exploding cartridge as power. This gun could shoot four hundred rounds in a minute. In World War I, some armies used gas-pressure guns, and others used earlier types. John Moses Browning, an American, invented a recoil-powered, water-cooled automatic gun in 1910 that he continued to perfect before America entered the war in 1917. This water-cooling system kept these guns from overheating so the soldiers could fire them continuously.

Flamethrowers used liquid fuel to shoot a jet of fire. Portable flamethrowers used in combat were a WWI innovation. Only the Germans had them when the war began, and theirs did not work well. However, German officer Bernhard Reddemann, a fire chief before the war, worked with other firemen in his unit to improve the flamethrower and use it in battle charges. Flamethrowers had backpacks with two cylinders, one holding nitrogen gas and the other a flammable liquid. The gas forced the liquid out through a pipe that led to a gun with an igniter. When the soldier pressed the trigger, flames shot out.

A German soldier holding a "stick hand" grenade [87]

Grenades—small hand-thrown bombs—had been part of warfare from ancient times. New technology with explosives made grenades a defining weapon of World War I. Some of the grenades used in WWI exploded on impact. Others had a timed fuse. Most weighed around a pound. The French, British, and Germans had "bomb squads" of around nine men. Some carried the grenades, some were the throwers, and some carried bayonets in case they were attacked. The German "Stielhandgranate" or "stick hand grenade" had a long wooden handle and a pull cord. The British called them "potato mashers" because they looked like the kitchen tool.

Naval mines were self-explosive devices placed to blow up enemy ships and submarines. In WWI, the mines were often positioned to guard ports, leaving a "safe" zone for friendly ships to sail through. Enemy ships did not know exactly where the safe zone was, so captains avoided entering enemy ports for fear of hitting a mine. Some types of mines rested on the seabed in shallower water. "Moored mines" had a tether tying them to the seabed. If an enemy ship bumped into a mine, it exploded, and the ship usually sank.

A depth charge was a canister of explosives that a ship's crew would drop if they knew an enemy submarine was nearby. A fuse would go off at a certain depth from the surface when it fell into the water. Even if it did not hit the submarine directly, shock waves would damage its instruments and joints, forcing it to the surface. Then, the ship could fire on the submarine with its big guns.

What Innovations in Communications Changed Things?

Field telephones were used by command units to communicate with the soldiers on the front lines. The telephone had only been invented four decades earlier, so it was an evolving technology. The US Army built two thousand miles of telephone lines stretching across the Western Front, using poles installed by the French. Shells and bullets often damaged the lines. Another problem was that the Germans had the technology to listen in. Consequently, other communication methods supplemented telephones.

Radiotelegraphy and spark-gap transmitters sent messages by Morse code, using a combination of long and short signals of light or sound to represent letters. Ships mostly used radio (or wireless) telegraphy to communicate with each other. An electric spark produced the radio waves used by spark-gap transmitters. The sender used a key to switch the transmitter on and off, which created radio-wave pulses. The receiver listened to "beeps" in earphones and translated the Morse code into written words.

Hydrophones were invented by the Allies in WWI and used by ships to discover if submarines were lurking under the surface. Ceramic hydrophones were placed in the water to listen for the engine sounds of a submarine. When underwater, changes in pressure cause some ceramics to produce a slight electrical current. Sound waves create changes in pressure, so a hydrophone converts the underwater noises from a submarine into electrical signals. Hydrophones can also pick up other underwater noises, like whales singing or the distinctive cracking sounds of icebergs.

Dogs and carrier pigeons carried messages when technology was a challenge. Twenty thousand dogs carried messages across the Allied front in WWI. Since they were fast and close to the ground, it was hard for the enemy to see and shoot them. Depending on the breed and the terrain, a dog can run ten miles in an hour or two. Dogs also came in handy for catching the thousands of rats in the trenches.

British messenger dogs with their trainer in France, 1918 [38]

The Allies used stray dogs from animal shelters, and hundreds of families donated their pets for the war effort. In 1917, the British established the War Dog School of Instruction, where they taught dogs how to deliver first aid supplies to wounded soldiers and to deliver messages. The dogs became beloved companions for the soldiers in the trenches. Sometimes, the soldiers volunteered to carry messages rather than putting the dogs in harm's way.

Carrier pigeons (homing pigeons) could find their way to their home base over an astonishing distance, even as far as a thousand miles. In less than an hour, they could carry a message over one hundred miles. The British started with sixty pigeons at the beginning of the war. They were so helpful that the British had twenty thousand pigeons delivering messages by the war's end.

A pigeon named Cher Ami was the hero of the Meuse-Argonne Offensive. The Germans had surrounded the American 77th Division, and the men desperately needed help but could not reach the Allies by telephone or radio. Cher Ami was their only pigeon, and they sent him off. Despite getting shot in the leg and breast, Cher Ami bravely flew on and reached the Allies, who rescued the Americans.

Roundup Activity: Fill in the Blank

Choose from the answers below. Check the back of the book to see if you are correct.

The British invented _____ to travel over trenches and shoot artillery from a protected cabin. The _____ _____ flew the first airplane, taught American officers how to fly them, and demonstrated how to shoot machine guns from an airplane. World War I's best fighter pilot, who shot down eighty planes, had the nickname the _____ _____. German _____ used balloon technology to drop bombs on cities. The Allies used both _____ and steam locomotives to pull trains on the trench railways. The Germans released _____ _____ on the Allies in the Second Battle of Ypres. Small, handheld bombs called _____ were a common weapon of WWI. Ships used _____ _____ to disable or destroy submerged submarines. _____ helped them know if submarines were nearby. _____ and pigeons carried messages when technology was a challenge.

chlorine gas	depth charges	dogs	grenades
horses	hydrophones	Red Baron	tanks
Wright brothers		Zeppelins	

Chapter 7: The United States Enters the Fray

America was a latecomer to World War I. It did not declare war until April 1917, almost three years into the war. Nevertheless, the United States tipped the scales for an Allied victory, ending the stalemate in the trenches. America sent fresh troops and financial support to the weary, war-torn front. American factories made millions of weapons and desperately needed supplies.

The war also transformed America into a major player on the world stage.

Why Did the United States Remain Neutral for the First Three Years?

President Wilson's official policy was "neutrality in thought as well as action." For one thing, America did not have much of a military when the war started. Its army only had 133,000 men. The National Guard had another 181,620. By contrast, the Central Powers had nearly twenty-two million soldiers.

Besides the lack a formidable army, most American people did not want to get involved. "It's not our battle!" they would say. "Those Europeans are always fighting about something. It has nothing to do with us!"

This is known as *isolationism*, the idea that a country should focus on problems at home rather than get involved in other countries' issues. If the United States stayed neutral, it could keep critical economic ties. Most Americans still wanted to trade with both the Allies and Central Powers, so it was to their advantage to stay friendly with both sides.

Another factor was the "Third Wave of Immigration" from 1880 to 1914. It brought over twenty million newcomers from eastern and southern Europe to America's shores, increasing America's population by about 25 percent. People flooded in from the Balkans, Italy, Poland, and Russia to escape Europe's political turmoil and find jobs in America's factories. The newcomers came from countries on both sides of the war. What would happen if the United States went to war? Would the recent immigrants be loyal to America or to their land of origin?

Why Did the United States Join the War in 1917?

In 1915, a German submarine torpedoed the *Lusitania*, a British passenger ship sailing from New York to Great Britain. The ship sank in only eighteen minutes, killing 128 American men, women, and children. A total of 1,197 people died, even tiny babies. Between January and April 1917, German submarines sank ten American merchant ships. The seas were no longer safe, even for neutral countries.

The Germans sank the Lusitania. [39]

In January 1917, British intelligence discovered that Germany was trying to strike an alliance with Mexico. The Germans promised to help Mexico regain territories it had lost to the United States before the Civil War. If the plan worked, America could lose parts of Arizona, New Mexico, and Texas. It was one thing when the war was on the other side of the Atlantic. Now, Germany was directly threatening American soil. Neutrality was off the table.

President Woodrow Wilson found himself in a difficult position. He had won reelection by keeping America out of the war. Now, war was inevitable. He addressed the nation on April 2, 1917:

> "There are serious, very serious, choices of policy to be made, and made immediately ... The present German submarine warfare against commerce is a warfare against mankind ... American ships have been sunk, American lives taken ... Neutrality is no longer feasible or desirable where the peace of the world is involved ... The world must be made safe for democracy."[i]

Four days later, America declared war on Germany. Once the United States joined the war, multiple other nations joined the Allies, like China, Costa Rica, Cuba, Greece, Honduras, and Nicaragua. Cuba sent men to fight. Greece provided a refuge for the exiled Serbians and fought fiercely against the Bulgarians and Turks. China sent laborers to the front to support the Allies. For Nicaragua, Honduras, and Costa Rica, declaring war was largely symbolic, but they did keep Germany from getting a foothold in Central America.

President Woodrow Wilson, 1915 [40]

---

[i] "Joint Address to Congress Leading to a Declaration of War Against Germany (1917)," National Archives, accessed March 3, 2025, https://www.archives.gov/milestone-documents/address-to-congress-declaration-of-war-against-germany.

How Did America Mobilize Its Resources for War?

Going to war meant the United States had to increase the size of its tiny army quickly. Why did such a large nation have a small army? The United States had the world's largest economy but wasn't a political superpower yet. Americans did not see the need for a massive number of troops. The Atlantic and Pacific oceans acted as natural barriers. Airplanes were not yet flying over oceans. Canada was not a threat, and Mexico was distracted by a civil war.

Now, America was facing off against the Central Powers. Germany had eleven million men in its armed forces. Austria-Hungary had 7.8 million soldiers, and the Ottoman Empire's army was 2.9 million. The United States had to build its military at lightning speed. Congress came through, approving an astounding three billion dollars to fund the new "million-man army." The million-man army was actually closer to five million men. The United States rose to the seemingly insurmountable task of recruiting and drafting millions of men. What's more, it needed to train these men immediately and provide them with weapons and uniforms.

Eventually, America spent about fifteen billion dollars on the war (370 billion in today's money). Where did the money come from? Most came from income taxes. During the Civil War, President Lincoln introduced a 3 percent income tax to pay for the war. Americans hated the income tax so much that Congress later eliminated it for most people. Instead, it taxed beer, wine, liquor, and tobacco. That covered 90 percent of the costs of running the country.

Yet, as war loomed, Congress revived the income tax. Anyone who made less than $5,000 a year (most Americans) had to pay a 2 percent tax. By the end of the war, taxes soared. Anyone making less than $5,000 a year had to pay a 6 percent tax. People making over $300,000 a year had to pay half their salary in income taxes.

While mobilizing its military, the United States wanted to clarify one thing to the Allies. Most Americans, especially those in charge, did not want Europe to return to the status quo when the war ended. They knew the war would topple empires. Yet, instead of building new empires, the United States wanted democracy to succeed. America also had an independent streak and didn't want to submit to European leadership while fighting.

WWI recruitment poster [41]

The United States basically said, "We have declared war on Germany, but that doesn't mean we're formally joining the Allies. We are an 'Associated Power.' That means we will fight *with* you, but not *for* you. We're still calling the shots when it comes to our military. We decide what our objectives are in this war, and we decide the strategies."

The French frowned. They had assumed they would merge the American troops with their brigades until the United States drafted and trained enough men for an independent army. The British sniffed at the new soldiers being trained in America. "Everyone knows the British have the world's best army training program," they said. "America's new recruits need to go through *our* training program. Then we'll assign them to our experienced units, and they can learn how war is properly done!"

Nevertheless, President Wilson put his foot down. Many Americans were not entirely on board with going to war. They certainly did not want their soldiers fighting under another country's flag. Wilson wanted to be at the table when the war was over, shaping what peace would look like. America's army needed independence for the United States to have a say in the war's end.

Wilson also needed Americans to rally behind the war effort. To encourage that, he formed a propaganda unit called the Committee on Public Information. **Propaganda** is (sometimes misleading) information widely spread to convince people to take a particular point of view or support a political effort. The Committee on Public Information plastered posters on walls and handed out pamphlets. They wrote newspaper articles, gave speeches, and produced movies glorifying America's role in the war: "Germany and the other Central Powers are in league with the devil! They're destroying democracy! The Germans are the enemies of civilization!"

German Americans had always been proud of their heritage. Now, they altered their last names so they wouldn't sound so German. Americans also renamed things that had German names. They called dachshunds "liberty pups," and "liberty cabbage" was the new name for sauerkraut.

To feed the millions of American soldiers and help feed the European Allies, Americans also needed to eat less, especially "luxuries" like meat. Herbert Hoover, who later became America's president, led the United States Food Administration. He promoted "Meatless Monday" and "Wheatless Wednesday." Patriotic Americans were urged to start "liberty gardens" to grow their own vegetables. Americans responded enthusiastically, cutting how much they ate by 15 percent and doubling the amount of food sent to the European Allies.

American soldiers in a canteen in France [48]

Two million young men volunteered at recruiting stations, yet it wasn't nearly enough. The US War Department began drafting soldiers. During the Civil War, the draft had left a sour taste because wealthy families could pay for someone else to substitute for their sons. This time, all men between twenty-one and thirty had to register for the draft. They couldn't hire substitutes or pay for exemptions. As the war continued, the United States needed more soldiers. The War Department increased the draft to all males between eighteen and forty-five. Over twenty-four million men registered for the draft, and from those, almost three million were called up to fight in the war.

Once recruited or drafted, training began for the new United States soldiers in over thirty training camps in America and France. They needed to get in good physical shape and learn how to drill, follow orders, work as a unit, use gas masks, lay barbed wire, and shoot various weapons. France and Britain sent officers to help train the American "doughboys" (the nickname for American soldiers). The factories had not produced enough rifles yet, so the recruits had to practice with fake wood guns. Training usually lasted six months, meaning that most of the United States military did not begin fighting on the front until early 1918.

Meanwhile, in Europe, half the French army had mutinied and refused to fight any longer. The French commander-in-chief resigned, and General Philippe Pétain replaced him. His strategy was to do as little as possible until more tanks and the American soldiers arrived. He allowed his men to rest, refusing to order any new attacks on the Germans.

What Was the Role of American Women in WWI?

Over sixteen thousand American women sailed to Europe with the American Expeditionary Forces. They worked near the front lines as telephone operators, nicknamed "Hello Girls." They also worked as clerks and operated canteens, serving food to the soldiers. Twenty-one thousand American nurses worked with the American Red Cross or Army Nurse Corps. Ten thousand were at field hospitals near the front lines in Italy and France. Others served at base hospitals in Britain and France. Other young women served in the US Navy as radio operators, translators, and truck drivers.

The US Navy actively recruited women for WWI in non-combat roles. [48]

With millions of men joining the military, American women stepped in to fill their shoes back home, working at factories and tending farms. Before the war, only about 20 percent of American women worked outside the home. Now, women labored in factories around the clock, seven days a week, to produce guns, tanks, and uniforms for America's massive new military. The "Women's Land Army" plowed fields, planted and harvested crops, and drove tractors.

How Did the American Expeditionary Force Help Win WWI?

President Wilson appointed General John J. Pershing to command the American Expeditionary Force sent to Europe. Pershing's nickname was "Blackjack" because he commanded the "Buffalo Soldiers"—the all-Black Tenth Cavalry Regiment in the Spanish-American War (1898). In the hurry to get troops to France, the Americans did not wait for guns, tanks, or airplanes. They borrowed French and British equipment until the shipments arrived.

The United States' first major battle in World War I was in the poppy-covered fields of northern France. America's most experienced soldiers, the First Infantry Division, fought the *Battle of Cantigny* in May 1918. These men were part of America's tiny army before the war and had been in trenches with the French for two months. Now, General Pershing took them out of the trenches for "open warfare." The French looked on curiously. How would the "raw" Americans do?

Their assignment was to take the village of Cantigny from the Germans. This area had few trenches and no barbed wire. The Germans held the high ground and had balloons from which to shoot. Nevertheless, the Americans captured Cantigny in thirty minutes, using a "rolling barrage" tactic. This involved sustained shooting for several minutes, followed by a charge of about a hundred yards. They repeated the barrage until they took the village captive.

The Germans didn't know what hit them. They were war-weary and used to the tired, half-hearted attacks from the British and French. However, they rallied and launched an all-out counterattack. Major Theodore Roosevelt Jr., another son of former President Theodore Roosevelt, led the 26th Regiment (part of the First Division) against the German troops. Although 199 soldiers were killed, the Americans won the battle, proving themselves to the French.

A week later, the US Fourth Marine Brigade and the Army's Third Brigade joined the French in a face-off against the Germans. The epic **Battle of Belleau Wood** in June 1918, a part of the Second Battle of the Marne, was legendary for the US Marines. The Marines had been an American fighting force since the American Revolution, but this was their first large-scale battle in France.

As the German soldiers approached through the woods, the Marine commander ordered, "Don't shoot until they are a hundred yards out!" The Marines were lying in shallow depressions they had dug, which protected them from most of the German fire. When the Marines opened fire, they mowed down the Germans at close range.

The survivors fled but rallied and returned to fight again. The fighting, mostly hand-to-hand combat, raged in the woods for almost a month. Although desperately outnumbered, the Marine "Devil Dogs" saved the day, pushing the Germans out of the woods and away from Paris. Yet, the battle killed over 1,800 American soldiers and wounded another 8,000.

During the **Hundred Days Offensive** in France, the **Battle of Saint-Mihiel** (September 1918) pitted 216,000 fighters from the American Expeditionary Forces and 48,000 French troops against a much smaller German army. This was the first time the Americans used the US Army Air Service. It was the war's largest air operation, with 1,481 American, British, French, and Italian airplanes.

The goal was to take the town of Saint-Mihiel, which the Germans had held from the beginning of the war. Major General George Patton rode on top of a tank in a major charge of 144 tanks. The Allied forces successfully put the Germans into retreat. Eleven days later, the **Meuse-Argonne Offensive** began, ending the war with a stunning victory by the Allies.

Tanks in the Battle of Saint-Mihiel"

How Did the War Change America?

World War I transformed the United States into a global power. It abandoned isolationism and took active leadership on the world stage. Its economy prospered as its factories manufactured the weapons and goods needed for war. The federal government increased its authority, and the income tax never went away. The women who had served on the front or in factories or farms at home were empowered. They finally got the right to vote two years after the war ended.

Roundup Activity: Review Questions

Check your answers in the back of the book.

1. Why did the United States stay neutral when WWI first began in 1914?

2. What two events led to the United States joining the war in 1917?

3. Why did the United States have such a small military before joining the war?

4. Why was the draft necessary?

5. What did the Committee on Public Education do?

6. What did American women serving in Europe in WWI do?

7. What was the United States' first major battle in WWI? Who won?

8. In what battle was the war's largest air operation? How many airplanes did the Allies have in that battle?

Chapter 8: Revolution and the End of the War

The Russian Revolution sent shock waves through the Allies. When the Communists came to power, Russia pulled out of the war. Russia had the world's largest military, and losing the Russian army struck a blow to the Allies. What triggered the Russian Revolution? Why did the Russian people revolt against the imperial court? How did Vladimir Lenin and the Bolsheviks take power? This chapter unwraps how it all played out.

Fortunately for the Allies, it wasn't a fatal blow when Russia pulled out in March 1918. The United States had entered the war, and its troops were arriving in Europe just as the Russian soldiers were leaving. The Allies prevailed. One by one, the Central Powers collapsed, beginning with Bulgaria, then the Ottoman Empire, Austria-Hungary, and finally, Germany.

What Events Led Up to the Russian Revolution of 1917?

In the years before the war, Russia's people became increasingly dissatisfied with their lives and government. Their tsars (emperors) had been oppressive and cruel. Russia's upper classes held the power and wealth. Until 1861, most Russians were peasants, farming land they didn't own. This system, in which the nobility owned most of the land and the peasants, or "serfs," farmed it, was called *serfdom*. Twenty-three million people in Russia were serfs.

The serfs "belonged" to the lords—the upper-class landowners and had limited rights. For instance, they couldn't get married without permission from their lord. They couldn't own property or have a business. They weren't allowed to move away.

In 1861, Russia eliminated serfdom in a new wave of reform. Most of Europe had gotten rid of it decades or even centuries earlier.

Russian farmers, early 1900s [45]

Now, the enormous tracts of land once owned by the lords were divided among the peasant farmers. However, the serfs did not get the land for free. They had to "buy" it by making payments to the former landowners for forty-nine years. These payments kept the farmers in poverty. Any profit they made from the land went to their former landlords. Sometimes, a bad harvest kept them from making their payments. It seemed impossible to be debt-free.

Meanwhile, the *Industrial Revolution* took hold in Russia. New technology transformed rural farm communities into urban industrial societies. Instead of working as farmers, many Russians now worked in factories in big cities. The populations of Moscow and St. Petersburg nearly doubled. The growing number of factory employees lived in filthy slums. Despite long hours, the wages were low.

Russia was one of Europe's poorest countries. Wars and bad harvests caused food shortages. Almost a half million Russians died from starvation from 1891 to 1892. Compared to most Western European nations, Russia was backward. It wasn't developing as quickly as Germany, Britain, and France. Russia's workers realized their government was corrupt, and their tsar did not seem to care. By contrast, America had been thriving as a democracy for more than a century, and some European nations were moving away from monarchies.

Nine years before World War I began, hundreds of Russians marched on Tsar Nicholas II's palace. They demanded more rights and better working conditions. The tsar was not in his palace, yet his guards followed standing orders and fired into the crowd. They killed or wounded at least a thousand people in the ***Bloody Sunday Massacre of 1905.*** In the coming weeks, the angry Russians revolted. The factory workers went on strike, joining Russia's farmers and soldiers to form a "soviet" council of workers.

In desperation, Nicholas II agreed to a new parliamentary form of government called a "***duma***," (something like a congress). Russia's State Duma had elected leaders (something new to Russia) to represent the people. Some representatives were peasant farmers or workers, another first for Russia. However, the first Duma only lasted seventy-three days. Tsar Nicholas dissolved it when the Duma demanded reforms. The people tried again with a second Duma in 1907; it lasted a little over three months before Nicholas dissolved it. The third Duma survived five years but had no representatives from the lower classes. The fourth Duma lasted through the war until 1917 but with little power.

Why Did the Russian People Eject Their Tsar and Establish Communism?

World War I made life even harder for Russia's working-class people as it drove up the prices of food and other necessities. Consequently, the Marxist Bolshevik movement strengthened, promoting "peace, land, and bread." Their leader was Vladimir Lenin. Russia's losses in World War I made matters worse. The Russian military was no match for Germany's war technology, modern weapons, and high discipline. Russia lost more men than any country had ever lost in a war.

Vladimir Lenin, 1917 [46]

On the Eastern Front, the Russians faced off against Austria-Hungary and Germany. The Central Powers destroyed the Russian regiments. In Russia, mobs formed, blaming the tsar, his wife, and their spiritual advisor, Rasputin. They threatened to shut Tsarina Alexandra in a convent and dethrone the tsar.

What did they have against the tsar's wife? Alexandra's mother was a British princess, the daughter of the British Queen Victoria. However, her father was a German grand duke and a cousin of Germany's emperor, Wilhelm II. The Russians skipped over the British part and focused on Alexandra's German heritage. Furthermore, the Russians felt the tsarina was too political. Alexandra was against reform and counseled her husband against it.

In 1915, things were so bad on the Eastern Front that Tsar Nicholas decided to take personal command. He traveled to Mogilev (in today's Belarus), yet his presence on the front did not help Russia. It continued losing to the Germans, and now Nicholas was blamed.

Meanwhile, he was far from his capital, where he had left his wife in charge. That wasn't going well. The Russians felt that Rasputin had too much power over Alexandra. They also suspected she had German sympathies. Alexandra's only son, Alexei, had hemophilia, and she was sure Rasputin could heal him. Yet, several Russian nobles murdered

Rasputin in December 1916.

By early 1917, Russia had lost 1.7 million soldiers in World War I. The winter had been harsh, crippling the railroads. Supplies weren't reaching the front, and the people in Russia were starving. In the icy weather, they had little food and no fuel to heat their homes. In February 1917, riots broke out in the capital of Petrograd. People smashed bakery windows to get bread. Holding red banners, they marched through the streets yelling, "Down with the tsar! Down with the war!"

The police shot at the unarmed protesters, and riots broke out. The Russian military stationed in Petrograd mostly sided with the protesters.

On the front, Tsar Nicholas received misinformation that the rebellion in Petrograd had been successfully subdued. In reality, mobs gathered in the street again in early March 1917. The police shot and killed over two hundred protesters. This sparked a mutiny of the Russian army regiments in Petrograd. Sixty thousand soldiers joined the protesters and burned down the police stations.

Russian soldiers fire on tsar's police, March 1917 [47]

Tsar Nicholas had no choice but to resign. He named his brother, Michael, as Russia's next tsar. Michael said he would only be tsar if the people voted for the monarchy to continue, which didn't happen. The Russians had a temporary government led by the Duma and the Soviet Council. The Duma warned Alexandra to leave with her children immediately. Yet, she refused to leave until her husband returned from the front. It took Nicholas a week to travel home. He knew he needed to get his family out of Russia for their safety, but where would they go?

Tsar Nicholas and his wife Alexandra were both first cousins of King George V of England. They hoped to escape there. On March 19, 1917, the British government said the royals could come to England, although going to a neutral country was a better idea. The British offered to send a ship to pick up the Russian royal family.

However, King George interfered. He knew his British subjects despised Alexandra because she was German-born. The British hated the Germans so much that King George had changed his surname to "Windsor" from the German "Saxe-Coburg-Gotha." He was afraid that bringing the Russian royal family to Britain would remind his subjects of his own German heritage. What if Britain revolted? Furthermore, he needed to smooth things over with Russia. America had not joined the war yet. If Russia pulled out of the war, the Allies were sunk. So, King George chose to leave his cousins in Russia.

Other European countries also hesitated to rescue the Russian Romanov family. Nicholas and his family waited in the remote town of Tobolsk in Siberia, hoping for a miracle.

Tsar Nicholas II and his family [48]

In November 1917, Vladimir Lenin led the leftist Bolshevik Revolution. It put farmers, workers, and soldiers in control of the new Communist government, with Lenin at its head as dictator. Civil war raged for the next few months between the Bolshevik Red Army and the

White Army, which represented an unlikely mix of people. The White Army had no common ideology. Some supported the tsar, and some supported a democratic socialism different from Lenin's Communism. The civil war continued through WWI and several years after.

Although the Bolsheviks were not entirely in control of Russia, they withdrew from World War I in March 1918. This meant Germany no longer had to fight on two fronts, so more German soldiers headed to the Western Front.

The miracle rescue never came for Tsar Nicholas and his family. In July 1918, the Bolsheviks murdered Nicholas, his wife, and all his children.

How Did the Central Powers Collapse and Request an Armistice?

Bulgaria was the first major nation of the Central Powers to surrender. Bulgaria had declared itself neutral when the war first began. It was still reeling from the Second Balkan War, which had been a miserable disaster. The Bulgarians planned to keep their heads down and wait it out. However, both the Allies and the Central Powers tried to entice Ferdinand I, Bulgaria's tsar, to join them. He finally joined the Central Powers in 1915, despite never forgiving Wilhelm II for smacking his bottom once. Ferdinand wanted to get back the land he'd lost to Serbia in the Second Balkan War. Germany sweetened the pot with an extravagant financial loan.

Bulgaria's involvement in World War I was on the Balkan Front. Ferdinand's first act in the war was to invade Serbia on October 14, 1915. His coordinated attack with Germany and Austria-Hungary sent the Serbians into the Great Retreat. The Central Powers occupied Serbia for the rest of the war, and the Bulgarians committed horrible atrocities against the Serbians.

The Balkan States [49]

However, as we mentioned earlier, Serbia defeated Bulgaria in the Vardar Offensive after Austria-Hungary and Germany withdrew from the Balkans. In the September 1918 **Armistice of Salonica**, Ferdinand abdicated his throne and disbanded his army.

After the **Ottoman Empire** suffered a bitter loss to Britain in the Middle East, the Ottoman's Grand Vizier Talaat Pasha met with the German and Bulgarian leaders in September 1918. He concluded that the Central Powers could not win the war. Talaat Pasha resigned and was replaced by General Ahmed Izzet Pasha, who contacted the British two days later. The British were more than happy to work out a deal. General Pasha also asked for negotiations with France, but it delayed in answering. The British wanted to keep their foothold in the Middle East and sped up negotiations to keep France out of the decisions.

The British had a list of demands, but the only two they really cared about were keeping their forts in the Dardanelles Strait and having free passage through the Bosphorus Strait. These straits were necessary for their shipping trade on the Black Sea. The Ottomans agreed almost immediately to most of the British demands. On October 30, 1918, the British and Ottomans signed the **Armistice of Mudros**, and the Ottoman Empire was out of the war.

Austria-Hungary was in a dismal state. The war had collapsed its economy, and its people were starving. Emperor Franz Joseph had died in 1916, and his grand-nephew, Karl I, was emperor. Now, two years later, the union between Hungary and Austria was falling apart. No one wanted a monarchy anymore. They were tired of fighting. For one thing, they had no bullets. They also knew the Allies were winning. Why die for a war they were doomed to lose?

On October 14, 1918, the Austro-Hungarian foreign minister asked the Allies for an armistice. Two days later, Karl I announced his idea, called the ***People's Manifesto***. The empire would become five kingdoms: Austria, Bohemia, Croatia, Hungary, and Polish Galicia. He was too late. Reform was no longer an option. The diverse people groups in the empire wanted to carve out their own destiny. The Slavic people wanted to unite with Serbia, and the Czechs and Slovaks wished to form a new, independent country.

On October 17, 1918, the Hungarians voted to end the union with Austria. They recalled all Hungarian troops from the front lines. Although Karl I never officially abdicated his throne, he declared that the people of Austria and Hungary had the right to determine the form of government they wanted. While this was being sorted out, Austria asked Italy for an armistice on October 29. Italy agreed to the ***Armistice of Villa Giusti*** with Austria-Hungary, which became official on November 4. By mid-November, the empire was divided into the Republic of German Austria and the Hungarian Democratic Republic.

Germany was the only Central Powers nation still in the war. Its struggle on the Western Front had not been going well. American troops had poured into France. In the Hundred Days Offensive, over a million German soldiers were killed, captured, or wounded. The Allies had launched attacks on two flanks of the Western Front, enclosing the Germans in a pincher movement.

The Allies blockaded the German supply lines, cutting off their food and weapons. Both the Germans and Allies were fighting the Spanish flu, but the German soldiers had almost nothing to eat. "It's hopeless!" the German first quartermaster general, Erich Ludendorff, told Kaiser Wilhelm II on September 29, 1918. "I can't guarantee that the front will hold for another two hours!"

On October 5, 1918, the German chancellor, Prince Maximilian of Baden (Max von Baden), messaged President Wilson. "We want to negotiate terms."

Wilson responded on October 23, noting that three things had to happen:
1) German troops had to leave all the territories they were occupying.
2) All submarine activities had to stop.
3) Kaiser Wilhelm II had to abdicate.

Unfortunately, Prince Maximilian was fighting the Spanish flu and had fallen into a coma. Ten days later, Maximilian was somewhat functional again. He was dismayed to discover that while he was unconscious, Austria-Hungary and the Ottomans had pulled out of the war. Germany was on its own.

It got worse. The German fleet mutinied, and German workers and soldiers revolted against the government. Maximilian desperately reached out to President Wilson to resume negotiations.

Wilson replied on November 6: "Okay, we'll discuss a truce. But you took too long. Now, you're going to have to pay reparations."

Sweat poured down Maximilian's face. President Wilson insisted that Wilhelm II abdicate, but the kaiser refused: "I'll abdicate as emperor, but I want to be king of Prussia." Prussia took up two-thirds of Germany's territory, so being king meant Wilhelm would still hold a lot of power. Also, Germany's constitution said that the emperor of Germany was also the king of Prussia. Wilhelm had to be both or neither.

Prince Maximillian messaged President Wilson on November 9 that Wilhelm II was giving up both titles. Maximillian resigned from his own position that same day, and Wilhelm went into exile in the Netherlands on November 10.

Yet, there was still a problem. The negotiations had only been between Germany and the United States. France, Britain, and Italy were offended that they had been left out of the loop. "He's making promises and demands we haven't agreed to!" they said of President Wilson.

Wilson responded, "Let me hear from the war chiefs. What do they think?"

Douglas Haig, commander of the British forces, recommended a more moderate approach. If Germany retreated from France, Belgium, and Luxembourg, the Allies could declare victory. He thought Germany needed to keep its army to protect against a possible Communist threat from Russia. On the other hand, General Ferdinand Foch of France wanted Germany to surrender most of its weaponry and for Allied forces to be stationed in Germany. America's General Pershing pushed for a total surrender from Germany, not just an armistice.

The final terms of the armistice were that Germany had to immediately stop shooting and retreat from France, Belgium, and Luxembourg. They also had to give up Alsace-Lorraine, a territory in France that Germany had taken in 1871 after the Franco-Prussian War. Germany had to hand over thousands of airplanes, tanks, locomotives, machine guns, and other weaponry.

Allied officers celebrate the Armistice at an abandoned German canteen. [50]

The *Armistice of Compiègne* was official at 11 a.m. on November 11, 1918. World War I was over. The bells of Paris rang. German soldiers climbed out of their trenches, bowed to the Allies, and walked away. Eerie silence broken by laughter and cheers replaced the constant sound of gunfire. Robert Casey of Battery C, 124th Field Artillery Regiment, 33rd Division, wrote down his thoughts:

> "And this is the end of it. In three hours, the war will be over. It seems incredible even as I write it. I suppose I ought to be thrilled and cheering. Instead, I am merely apathetic and incredulous ... There is some cheering across the river—occasional bursts of it as the news is carried to the advanced lines. For the most part, though, we are in silence ... With all is a feeling that it can't be true. For months we have slept under the guns ... We cannot comprehend the stillness."[i]

---

[i] "Armistice," The National WWI Museum and Memorial, accessed March 3, 2025, https://www.theworldwar.org/learn/about-wwi/armistice.

Chapter 9: The Treaties: A New Map of Europe and the World

Once World War I finally ground to a halt, the countries involved had to hash out treaties. Yes, they had all signed armistices, but an armistice is only a promise to stop fighting. By contrast, a treaty is a formal agreement between two or more nations. It spells out what the future will look like. Each side makes promises that are "ratified," or approved and agreed to. This chapter explores the treaties between the Allies and the defeated Central Powers.

The Treaty of Versailles (June 1919)

Leaders from the "Big Four" (the United States, Great Britain, France, and Italy) met at the Paris Peace Conference in January 1919 to discuss several questions. What should the terms be for the defeated Central Powers? How would they move forward with Austria-Hungary, Bulgaria, Germany, and Turkey? No representatives from the Central Powers were invited. Russia was also not there. It had already negotiated peace terms with Germany when it pulled out of the war during the Russian Revolution.

President Wilson of the United States pushed for a new world order. He wanted to form an international organization to help solve the root causes of the war. He felt that all nations should reduce their military and weapons. In addition, minorities should have the opportunity to decide their destinies.

The Europeans looked at each other, their eyebrows raised. "He's too idealistic! It'll never work!" they whispered. "How would we ever put his principles into actual policy?" Instead, France had its way with harsh terms for Germany. Germany had started the war in Western Europe. Now, it had to accept responsibility and make things right. Germany must give back the land it stole from France decades earlier. It had to pay **reparations** (money or other help for people who have been wronged). Moreover, Germany had to reduce its military to only 100,000 men. It had to limit its navy to smaller ships and give up its air force, submarines, tanks, heavy artillery, and poison gas. Germany had to allow Allied inspectors into its factories to ensure it wasn't producing banned weaponry.

The Big Four: Lloyd George of Great Britain, Orlando of Italy, Clemenceau of France, and President Wilson of the United States [51]

Germany's humiliating terms in the treaty, signed on June 28, 1919, failed to deal with the underlying causes of the war. The reparations placed a crushing economic burden on the country. Its bitter and resentful people were vulnerable to Adolf Hitler's Nazi ideology. Ultimately, the Treaty of Versailles paved the way to World War II two decades later.

The Treaty of Saint-Germain (September 1919)

The next treaty was the Treaty of Saint-Germain with Austria. It was complicated because the Austro-Hungarian Empire had collapsed, splitting into two nations immediately after the war. Now, more divisions loomed. Instead of working out terms with one nation, the Allies had to sort out what the new countries were and make treaties with all of them.

First, the treaty recognized that the Austro-Hungarian Empire had dissolved. Hungary was now on its own. Other new countries pulled out of Austria-Hungary, as well. Poland, the Yugoslav Kingdom of Serbs, Croats, and Slovenes (later renamed Yugoslavia), and Czechoslovakia were now separate, independent nations.

The war began because the Serbs in Bosnia wanted freedom from Austria. They and many Slavic people now had that in the Yugoslav Kingdom. Yet, the Slavs had multiple ethnic groups. They still had to work things out among themselves, and it did not go well. The Slavic situation has been a simmering pot of trouble to this day.

Britain had promised Italy that it would get new territory from the Austro-Hungarian Empire if it joined the Allies. The Allies made good on that promise in the Treaty of Saint-Germain. They gave Italy bits and pieces of Austria, like Trentino, South Tyrol, Trieste, Istria, and some of the Dalmatian islands. Italy's northeastern area today was once part of Austria.

Austria, now a much smaller country, could only have an army of thirty thousand men. The treaty said Austria had to pay reparations but not how much. This never got resolved, so Austria never paid any money. However, the treaty also said Austria had to pay reparations with farm animals. Austria sent cows, horses, and sheep to Italy, the Yugoslav Kingdom, and Romania.

Europe after WWI [52]

The Treaty of Neuilly (November 1919)

The Allies met in Neuilly-sur-Seine, near Paris, France, to decide what to do about Bulgaria, which had fought with Austria-Hungary and Germany. As you may remember, when Bulgaria invaded Serbia, the Serbians fled over the Accursed Mountains. About 200,000 Serbians died in the Great Retreat in that horrible winter. The death toll from Bulgarian bombs, freezing weather, and starvation included thousands of women, children, and the elderly.

Once they chased off most of the Serbs, the Bulgarians and Austro-Hungarians took control of Serbia, dividing it between them. The Bulgarians also took the region south of Serbia, today's Macedonia. They aimed to wipe out all traces of the Serbian and Macedonian cultures. The Bulgarians put the remaining Serbs in internment camps. They made them do forced labor in an ethnic cleansing campaign. They shot many teachers, pastors, government leaders, and military men. They put the rest in concentration camps or sent them to Bulgaria to do forced labor.

It was time for the Bulgarians to pay the price for their war crimes. Bulgarian delegates attended the negotiations. However, they could not sit in all the meetings. The Allies made Bulgaria give its western territory to the new Yugoslav Kingdom of Serbs, Croats, and Slovenes. (The Yugoslav Kingdom was the land that had been Serbia, Bosnia, Croatia, Slovenia, Herzegovina, and Macedonia before the war.) In 1929, the Yugoslav Kingdom became Yugoslavia.

The Bulgarians had to give western Thrace to Greece. This part of Thrace was on the Aegean Sea, next to Greece's northeastern border. It meant Bulgaria lost priceless shipping trade. Bulgaria also had to give the region of Dobruja to Romania. Dobruja had fertile wheatfields and was on the Black Sea coast, so it was valuable land. Furthermore, the Allies forced the Bulgarians to limit their army to 20,000 men. They had to relinquish their warships, air force, and heavy artillery. They also had to pay the Allies reparations of 2.25 billion gold francs.

Why Was the League of Nations Formed? (January 1920)

President Wilson wanted to establish a "general association of nations" to help countries cooperate. He wanted it to act as a mediator between countries that had conflicts. He hoped to prevent a future world war. The Treaty of Neuilly also included the **Covenant of the League of Nations**. The covenant was a promise to work for international peace. Instead of fighting, it promoted peaceful ways to solve problems. The League of Nations was like a global club with rules for settling issues through diplomacy and discussions.

The Treaty of Trianon (June 1920)

The Allies met at the Trianon Palace in Versailles, France, to decide Hungary's fate. The result was devastating for Hungary. It lost two-thirds of its territory. Yet, Hungary was not in a position to argue. Things had gone from back to worse since the war ended. "Upper Hungary," or Slovakia, had pulled out of Hungary in 1918 and joined the Czech lands of Bohemia and Moravia (once in Austria). The new country was Czechoslovakia. It conspired with Romania and Yugoslavia to block food and fuel to Hungary.

Romania was neutral when World War I began but joined the Allies in 1916. It wanted to take back parts of Hungary with large Romanian populations living in them. Romania's main target in World War I was the Transylvania region in Hungary at the time. (Yes, it was that Transylvania, home of the bloody Vlad Dracula the Impaler in the fifteenth century, that inspired the Count Dracula story.) Romania successfully took Transylvania in the war but then lost it again. The Treaty of Trianon officially gave Transylvania to Romania.

When the Hungarians and Allies signed the Treaty of Trianon in June 1919, Hungary lost access to the Adriatic Sea. It was now landlocked, so it no longer had a navy. Hungary could have no more than 35,000 military men. Its northern and southern lands were now the new countries of Czechoslovakia and Yugoslavia. Romania had taken its western lands. Even Austria and Poland snipped off little pieces in the east and north. Hungary's population was about a third of what it had been before the war.

All the land above had been Hungary before the war.[58]

The Treaty of Sevres (July 1920)

This treaty dissolved what had once been Turkey's Ottoman Empire. It said that Turkey had to give up all its territory in the Middle East and North Africa. At its height (in the 1500s), the Ottoman Empire had ruled all the Middle Eastern lands bordering the Mediterranean Sea. It also controlled the Red Sea and part of the Persian Gulf. The treaty also said that Turkey had to give up its southeastern European territory. Basically, Turkey lost all territory that wasn't ethnically Turkish.

The Allies jostled each other to control former parts of the empire. Back in 135 CE, the Roman emperor Hadrian had defeated the Jewish state of Judaea. He renamed it Palaestina (Palestine). Under Ottoman rule, Palestine was the land between Lebanon and Egypt. In the Treaty of Sevres, the League of Nations placed Palestine and Transjordan (today's Jordan) under British rule. This was called the **Mandate for Palestine**. The agreement was that Britain would rule until the local people could rule on their own. However, Britain continued governing until after World War II.

Part of the agreement said that Palestine would be a national home for the Jewish people. Over the millennia, many Jews had left their homeland of Judaea for North Africa or Europe to escape persecution from the Romans, Muslims, and Crusaders. For the most part, the Ottoman Empire had allowed the Jews more freedom than other Islamic governments, so some Jews returned to their ancestral homeland.

Large numbers of Jews began coming back to Palestine in the 1800s. Antisemitism was becoming deadly in Europe and North Africa. They dreamed of rebuilding a Jewish nation built on democracy. About 94,000 Jews lived in Palestine at the beginning of World War I alongside Muslim Palestinians. Recent genetic testing shows that both groups are very closely related. Over 70 percent of Jewish men and half the Palestinian men inherited their Y chromosomes from common ancestors in the region in the past several thousand years.

The League of Nations also established the **Mandate for Syria and Lebanon**, which gave France control of the region north of Palestine.

The Ottoman leaders met and decided they had no choice but to accept the treaty. However, many Turks were trying to establish a new government at the end of WWI. The **Turkish War of Independence** had begun in 1919. These nationalists were outraged at the treaty's terms. They felt Turkey was being treated worse than Germany. The *Turkish National Movement* rebelled against the treaty. Finally, the Turkish government informed the Allies that it could not ratify the agreement.

Leaders of the Turkish Nationalist Movement, 1919 [64]

The Treaty of Lausanne (July 1923)

Almost five years had passed since WWI ended, but things still weren't sorted out with Turkey. Everyone had to go back to the drawing board. By this time, the Turkish Nationalist Movement had chased off its sultan and would soon install the first president of the new Republic of Turkey. Months of negotiations took place in Lausanne, Switzerland. This time, the primary discussions took place between the Turkish delegate, the British foreign secretary, and a representative from Greece.

An important article in this treaty gave ships from all countries the right to pass through the Turkish Straits (the Bosphorus Strait and Dardanelles) that connect the Aegean Sea to the Black Sea. The treaty recognized Turkey's new government but said that Turkey had to protect its Christian minority and Greece had to protect its Muslim minority. Turkey and Greece had been in conflict over where the border between the two countries lay, and the Lausanne Treaty spelled that out. Turkey did not challenge the Middle Eastern arrangements of the earlier Treaty of Sevres.

Roundup Activity: Name That Treaty

Which treaty enacted the following measures? Check your answers in the back of the book.

1. Austria and Hungary were now separate. Austria had to give land to Italy and pay reparations in farm animals. _____

2. Bulgaria had to give its western territory to the new Yugoslav Kingdom of Serbs, Croats, and Slovenes. It also had to give western Thrace to Greece and the region of Dobruja to Romania. _____

3. Germany had to pay reparations and reduce its military to 100,000 men. _____

4. Turkey had to allow ships from all countries to pass through the straits connecting the Aegean and Black seas. It clarified the border between Turkey and Greece. _____

5. Hungary lost two-thirds of its territory and had to limit its army to 35,000 men._____

6. The Ottoman Empire had to give up its Middle Eastern and North African territories and some European territories. _____

Conclusion

The Great War—the "war to end all wars"—was over. Now what? Did it really end all wars or even slow down conflict? What was the aftermath of World War I? What seeds of future conflicts did the events during and just after WWI sow? What happened when unresolved territorial disputes and minority grievances continued to simmer after the war? How did it influence the rise of fascism in Italy and the National Socialist Worker's Party in Germany? What about the Great Depression in the 1930s? How did World War I pave the way for this economic disaster?

Did World War I Slow Down Future Wars?

No. Within a year after WWI ended, Finland, Germany, Estonia, Latvia, Poland, Ukraine, and Ireland had revolutions. WWI not only failed to slow down conflict but also led to World War II only twenty-one years later. WWII was the world's deadliest war ever.

What Seeds of Future Wars Were Sown During and Immediately After WWI?

Unresolved territorial disputes fueled future wars. These included the new Eastern European borders, especially between Poland and Russia. When Austria-Hungary dissolved, Eastern Europe's borders were redrawn, and new countries were created. However, the new borders did not always account for ethnic groups. Some ethnic groups found themselves split off from the rest of the people who shared their language and culture.

When Turkey signed the Lausanne Treaty in 1923, a large Orthodox Christian Greek population (about 1.6 million) lived in Turkey, and about 400,000 Muslim Turks resided in Greece. There was already a lot of animosity between the two groups. The two countries agreed to swap their people. It was a type of ethnic cleansing. The theory was that if everyone in Turkey were Muslim, there wouldn't be religious conflict. People had to leave their houses with only what they could carry. It was traumatic for both the Greeks and Turks forced to migrate.

The Slavic countries like Serbia, Bosnia, and Croatia were lumped together in Yugoslavia, but now they experienced cultural tensions. The biggest divider was that some were Muslim, some Catholic, and some Orthodox Christian. Tension simmered for decades until, finally, it erupted into civil war in the 1990s. Bosnia and Herzegovina, Croatia, Kosovo, Montenegro, North Macedonia, and Serbia all broke off into independent countries.

What Is Fascism?
How Did WWI Spark This Ideology in Italy?

Fascism is an authoritarian political ideology that believes the most important thing for a country is its strength. Fascism sometimes promotes a country, race, or religion as superior to others. The citizens of fascist countries have little or no free speech. Fascism does not believe in equal rights for everyone.

Benito Mussolini was an Italian journalist who fought and was injured in WWI. He established Italy's National Fascist Party, which promoted *totalitarianism*, the idea that a country has only one political party led by a dictator who controls all public and private life.

After WWI, many of Italy's war veterans were disillusioned. They thought Italy would get more new territory after the war than it did. The war caused severe economic problems in Italy. Inflation was high, and there wasn't enough food. The people were restless and wanted change. Mussolini exploited the people's frustrations. He became Italy's prime minister in 1922 and, within five years, transformed Italy into a fascist dictatorship.

How Did WWI's Aftermath Lead to the Rise of the Nazi Party in Germany?

The brutal terms of the Treaty of Versailles left the German people seething in resentment. Like the Italians and other Europeans, they were suffering economically. It was incredibly humiliating to have lost the war.

Adolf Hitler had served in WWI and received the Iron Cross for bravery. He was wounded more than once and temporarily blinded by poison gas. When Germany surrendered, Hitler was outraged. He felt that the "backstabbing" Jews and socialists back home had betrayed the Germans by pushing to end the war.

Hitler played on the German people's disillusionment by promising to set things right for Germany. He established the National Socialist German Workers' Party (the Nazi Party), promising to restore Germany's strength and get back everything it had lost. He promoted the "Aryan master race," which he defined as the Germanic people. He denied citizenship to Jews, Black people, and Gypsies (a Romani people who originated in northern India). Although Hitler's beliefs were bizarre, his promises got people's attention, and he rose to power, setting the stage for World War II.

Did World War I Cause the Great Depression?

As mentioned above, most European countries suffered economically after the war. A decade after the war, the Great Depression hit in 1929 and lasted ten years. This global economic crash was modern history's worst financial disaster. It started when the stock market crashed, lowering the price of gold and creating a world crisis. Banks failed, and people lost their money that was in the banks. Meanwhile, the lack of rain in America's Midwest led to the "Dust Bowl." When their crops failed, people lost their farms. As businesses closed, unemployment skyrocketed.

Did WWI trigger the Great Depression? Obviously, there were other factors, like bad weather in America. Yet, Europe and other parts of the world were still reeling from World War I. Many countries had staggering war debt that made them vulnerable. The millions of men who died in the war meant there weren't enough workers. European farmland, towns, and cities had been destroyed.

The United States demanded that their European allies repay the money they'd borrowed during the war. The only way the Allies could repay the loans was to get money from Germany, which is why it had to pay such high reparations. The Allies got some money from Bulgaria, but the other countries that lost were already so poor it was useless to demand reparations. The war debt crippled the economies of many nations involved in the war.

In a bizarre turn of events, the American banks ended up loaning money to Germany so it could pay its reparations to the European Allies so the Allies could repay America. While Europe struggled to stay alive in the 1920s, America's banks were booming, but a lack of regulation led to bad business decisions. People got overconfident and started buying too many stocks. Meanwhile, Germany defaulted on its loan payments to America. When the price of stocks started going down, everyone tried to sell their stocks, and the banks crashed. Thus, World War I's financial aftermath triggered the Great Depression.

Hardly any good came out of World War I, and it brought a world of pain to people around the globe.

Answers

Roundup Activity Answers: Chapter 1

1. What countries were in the Triple Alliance and Triple Entente before WWI?
    a. Triple Alliance: Austria-Hungary, Germany, and Italy
    b. Triple Entente: France, Britain, and Russia

2. Why did Britain consider Germany its number one threat before WWI?
    Germany was building a vast navy. The only way to attack Britain was by water since it was an island nation.

3. What new battleship did Britain add in its arms race with Germany? What did Germany focus on in its navy?
    Britain added the dreadnought. Germany built a fleet of U-boat submarines.

4. What was Europe's most unstable region before WWI?
    The Balkans was Europe's most unstable region before WWI.

5. What was the Black Hand?
    The Black Hand was a secret society officially called Unification or Death. It was a military organization with the goal of liberating the Serbs outside Serbia who were still under the

Ottoman Empire or Austria-Hungary. They wanted to create a "Greater Serbia."

6. Why did Emperor Franz Joseph of Austria strike a deal with Hungary in 1867 to form a two-state empire?
Otto von Bismark had unified all the German states, except Austria, into the German Reich (Empire). Emperor Franz Joseph of Austria knew he was in danger of losing Hungary.

7. Why did Franz Joseph consider Sophie Chotek an unsuitable wife for his nephew, Franz Ferdinand?
Sophie Chotek wasn't royal.

Roundup Activity: Chapter 2

1) **Who was Archduke Franz Ferdinand, and why was he visiting Sarajevo in 1914?**

He was the next in line to be emperor of Austria-Hungary. He was visiting to inspect the military exercises.

2) **Why did the archduke bring his wife Sophie with him?**

It was their fourteenth wedding anniversary, and they wanted to spend it away from court.

3) **What did five of the six teenage assassins have in common?**

They had tuberculosis.

4) **Who trained and equipped the assassins? Why did they get involved?**

The Black Hand. They wanted to provoke a war with Austria-Hungary, hoping Russia would get involved and help them conquer Bosnia.

5) **What demand from Austria-Hungary did Serbia refuse to follow? Why?**

The one about Austria-Hungary being involved in the investigation of the assassination. Serbia's Prime Minister Pasic did not want an inquiry to reveal he knew about the assassination plot in advance. High-ranking Black Hand officials did not want it known that they were part of the plot.

Roundup Activity: Chapter 3

WWI: Life in the Trenches

Across

4. a cannon-like weapon that shot explosive shells
5. winners of the August 15, 1914 Battle of Cer
7. mystic advisor to Russia's royal family
10. a neutral country invaded by Germany
11. where WWI's first battle was fought on Aug 5, 1914
12. age of WWI's youngest soldier, a Serbian
13. Serbia's capital

Down

1. Germany's inexperienced teen soldiers
2. a common bowel problem in the trenches
3. what country did German invade first?
6. day in 1914 when both sides declared a truce
8. king of Belgium
9. location of a battle in France that began trench warfare

Roundup Activity: Chapter 4

October–November 1914, First Battle of Ypres
February–December 1916, Battle of Verdun
July–November 1916, Battle of the Somme
July–November 1917, Battle of Passchendaele
November–December 1917, Battle of Cambrai
August 8-11, 1918, Battle of Amiens
September–November 1918, Meuse-Argonne Offensive

Roundup Activity: Chapter 5

(T) 1. The Forgotten Fronts refer to the lesser-known Eastern, Italian, Balkan, Caucasus, and Middle Eastern fronts.

(T) 2. Some of the Forgotten Fronts were in the Middle East and northwestern Asia.

(F) 3. The Battles of Verdun and Somme took place on the Italian Front.

(F) 4. The German's "Schlieffen Plan" involved fighting Russia first and then attacking France.

(T) 5. Russia's Brusilov Offensive captured more territory than any other Allied offensive in World War I.

(T) 6. Italy scored two vital wins in the Battles of the Piave River.

(T) 7. The Great Retreat took the Serbians through the jagged Accursed Mountains.

(F) 8. The Ottoman Empire joined the war when Russian ships fired on Ottoman ships.

(T) 9. The Caucasus Campaign focused on the Black Sea's eastern shores.

(T) 10. The Ottomans' attempt to take the Suez Canal failed and caused them to lose Jerusalem and Gaza to the British.

Roundup Activity: Chapter 6

The British invented <u>tanks</u> to travel over trenches and shoot artillery from a protected cabin. The <u>Wright brothers</u> flew the first airplane, taught American officers how to fly them, and demonstrated how to shoot machine guns from an airplane. World War I's best fighter pilot, who shot down eighty planes, had the nickname, the <u>Red Baron</u>. German <u>Zeppelins</u> used balloon technology to drop bombs on cities. The Allies used both <u>horses</u> and steam locomotives to pull trains on the trench railways. The Germans released <u>chlorine gas</u> on the Allies in the Second Battle of Ypres. Small, handheld bombs called <u>grenades</u> were a common weapon of WWI. Ships used <u>depth charges</u> to disable or destroy submerged submarines. <u>Hydrophones</u> helped them know if submarines were nearby. <u>Dogs</u> and pigeons carried messages when technology was a challenge.

Roundup Activity: Chapter 7

1. Why did the United States stay neutral when WWI first began in 1914?

   It had an isolationist policy of not getting involved in other countries' political affairs.

2. What two events led to the United States joining the war in 1917?

   The German submarines kept sinking their ships.

   The Germans tried to get Mexico to fight the United States.

3. Why did the United States have such a small military before joining the war?

   Its isolationist policy kept it out of most wars. The Atlantic and Pacific acted as barriers. Canada wasn't a threat, and Mexico was busy with internal unrest.

4. Why was the draft necessary?

   They needed millions of men, but not enough volunteered.

5. What did the Committee on Public Education do?

   It spread propaganda to get Americans on board with the war effort.

6. What did American women serving in Europe in WWI do?

   They were telephone operators, nurses, canteen workers, clerks, radio operators, truck drivers, and translators.

7. What was the United States' first major battle in WWI? Who won?
   The Battle of Cantigny. America (and the Allies) won.
8. In what battle was the war's largest air operation? How many airplanes did the Allies have in that battle?
   The Battle of Saint-Mihiel had 1,481 American, British, French, and Italian airplanes.

Roundup Activity: Chapter 9

1. Austria and Hungary were now separate. Austria had to give land to Italy and pay reparations in farm animals. (Treaty of Saint-Germain)
2. Bulgaria had to give its western territory to the new Yugoslav Kingdom of Serbs, Croats, and Slovenes. It also had to give western Thrace to Greece and the region of Dobruja to Romania. (Treaty of Neuilly)
3. Germany had to pay reparations and reduce its military to 100,000 men. (Treaty of Versailles)
4. Turkey had to allow ships from all countries to pass through the straits connecting the Aegean and Black seas. It clarified the border between Turkey and Greece. (Treaty of Lausanne)
5. Hungary lost two-thirds of its territory and had to limit its army to 35,000 men. (Treaty of Trianon)
6. The Ottoman Empire had to give up its Middle Eastern and North African territories and some European territories. (Treaty of Sevres)

Here's another book by Enthralling History that you might like

Free limited time bonus

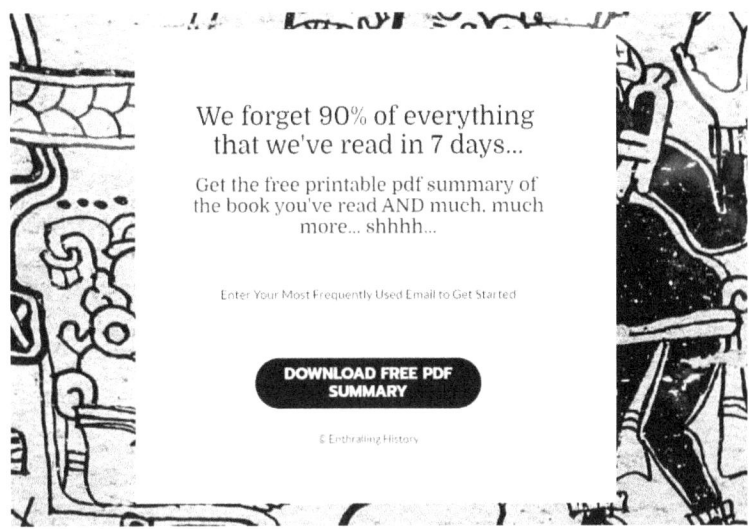

Stop for a moment. We have a free bonus set up for you. The problem is this: we forget 90% of everything that we read after 7 days. Crazy fact, right? Here's the solution: we've created a printable, 1-page pdf summary for this book that you're reading now. All you have to do to get your free pdf summary is to go to the following website: **https://livetolearn.lpages.co/enthrallinghistory/**

Or, Scan the QR code!

Once you do, it will be intuitive. Enjoy, and thank you!

Bibliography

Andrew, Christopher. "France and the Making of the Entente Cordiale." *The Historical Journal* 10, no. 1 (1967): 89-105. http://www.jstor.org/stable/2638063.

Australian War Memorial. "The Battle of Amiens: 8 August 1918." Accessed March 3, 2025. https://www.awm.gov.au/visit/exhibitions/1918/battles/amiens.

Gilbert, Martin. *The First World War: A Complete History*. Henry Holt & Company, 2004.

Grant, R. G. *World War I: The Definitive Visual History*. Smithsonian, 2024.

Imperial War Museums. "Voices of the First World War: The Submarine War." Accessed March 3, 2025. https://www.iwm.org.uk/history/voices-of-the-first-world-war-the-submarine-war#:~:text=Submarines%20played%20a%20significant%20military,encounter%20with%20a%20British%20ship.

Imperial War Museums. "Voices of the First World War: Zeppelins Over Britain." Accessed March 3, 2025. https://www.iwm.org.uk/history/voices-of-the-first-world-war-zeppelins-over-britain.

Keegan, John. *The First World War*. Vintage, 2000.

Kidd, Thomas S. *American History, Combined Edition: 1492-Present*. B&H Academic, 2019.

King, David C. *American History: A Visual Encyclopedia*. Penguin Random House, 2023.

Lloyd, Nick. *The Eastern Front: A History of the Great War, 1914-1918*. W. W. Norton & Company, 2024.

Lloyd, Nick. *The Western Front: A History of the Great War, 1914-1918*. W. W. Norton & Company, 2021.

Meyer, G. J. *A World Undone: The Story of the Great War, 1914 to 1918*. Bantam Dell, 2007.

National Archives. "Joint Address to Congress Leading to a Declaration of War Against Germany (1917)." Accessed March 3, 2025. https://www.archives.gov/milestone-documents/address-to-congress-declaration-of-war-against-germany.

National Archives. "Letters from the First World War: Part I." Accessed March 3, 2025. https://www.nationalarchives.gov.uk/education/resources/letters-first-world-war-1915/trenches-mostly-mere-boys/.

National Army Museum. "Battle of the Somme." Accessed March 3, 2025. Https://www.nam.ac.uk/explore/battle-somme.

O'Neill, Bill. *The World War 1 Trivia Book: Interesting Stories and Random Facts from the First World War.* LAK Publishing, 2019.

"The Great War: When the Americans Turned the Tide." *The New York Times,* June 26, 2014. https://www.nytimes.com/2014/06/27/world/europe/world-war-i-second-battle-of-the-marne.html#.

The National WWI Museum and Memorial. "Armistice." Accessed March 3, 2025. https://www.theworldwar.org/learn/about-wwi/armistice.

"The Teenage Soldiers of World War I." *BBC News,* November 11, 2014. https://www.bbc.com/news/magazine-29934965#:~:text=Technically%20the%20boys%20had%20to,Let's%20take%20him.%22.

Tuchman, Barbara W. *The Guns of August.* Ballantine Books, 1962.

Image Sources

1. https://commons.wikimedia.org/wiki/File:Triple_Alliance.png
2. https://commons.wikimedia.org/wiki/File:Wilhelm_II_in_Tangier.jpg
3. https://commons.wikimedia.org/wiki/File:HMSDreadnought_gunsLOCBain17494.jpg
4. Source map: TinodelaChanges: Flappiefh, CC BY-SA 3.0 <http://creativecommons.org/licenses/by-sa/3.0/>, via Wikimedia Commons: https://commons.wikimedia.org/wiki/File:Bosnia_and_Herzegovina_in_1911_map-fr.svg
5. https://commons.wikimedia.org/wiki/File:Black_Hand_Members.jpg
6. https://commons.wikimedia.org/wiki/File:Alfred-schmidt-cartoon-the-turks-power-in-europe-is-shaken-by-his-balkan-neighbours.jpg
7. https://commons.wikimedia.org/wiki/File:Sophie,_Duchess_of_Hohenberg.jpg
8. https://commons.wikimedia.org/wiki/File:Franz_Ferdinand_with_Princess_Sophie.jpg
9. https://commons.wikimedia.org/wiki/File:Grabez,_Cabrinovic,_Princip.jpg
10. Time Magazine cover, (1914), CC0, via Wikimedia Commons: https://commons.wikimedia.org/wiki/File:Franz_Ferdinand_%26_Sophie_in_Sarajevo.jpg
11. royaltyincolour, CC BY-SA 4.0 <https://creativecommons.org/licenses/by-sa/4.0>, via Wikimedia Commons: https://commons.wikimedia.org/wiki/File:Emperor_Franz_Joseph_I_of_Austria,_1892.png
12. Deutsch: K.u.k. Kriegspressequartier, Lichtbildstelle - Wien, Public domain, via Wikimedia Commons: https://commons.wikimedia.org/wiki/File:Inspizierung_der_MG-Kompanie_desSturmbataillons_durch_Exzellenz_Conrad_v.H%C3%B6tzendorf_(BildID_15624837).jpg
13. https://commons.wikimedia.org/wiki/File:Leopold_Graf_Berchtold_von_und_zu_Ungarschitz_1915_C._Pietzner.png
14. https://commons.wikimedia.org/wiki/File:Henriette_Caillaux_1914.jpg
15. Country labels added https://commons.wikimedia.org/wiki/File:Western_front_1914.jpg
16. National Library of Scotland, No restrictions, via Wikimedia Commons: https://commons.wikimedia.org/wiki/File:Reading_the_news_in_the_trenches_1000_yards_from_the_Bosch_present_positions_(4688659754).jpg

17 leon abraham, CC BY 3.0 <https://creativecommons.org/licenses/by/3.0>, via Wikimedia Commons: https://commons.wikimedia.org/wiki/File:Leon_abraham_WWI_soldier.jpg

18 State Library of New South Wales collection, No restrictions, via Wikimedia Commons: https://commons.wikimedia.org/wiki/File:In_the_Trenches,_Henry_Charles_Marshall_(17011773257).jpg

19 Photo zoomed in. Cassowary Colorizations, CC BY 2.0 <https://creativecommons.org/licenses/by/2.0>, via Wikimedia Commons: https://commons.wikimedia.org/wiki/File:German_and_British_troops_during_the_Christmas_Truce_of_1914_(27518523839).jpg

20 https://commons.wikimedia.org/wiki/File:A-Photo-of-German-Soldiers-During-the-Battle-of-Ypres-352029188390.jpg

21 Photo zoomed in. https://commons.wikimedia.org/wiki/File:The_Battle_of_the_Somme,_July-november_1916_Q4148.jpg

22 Photo zoomed in. https://commons.wikimedia.org/wiki/File:A_team_of_stretcher_bearers_struggle_through_deep_mud_to_carry_a_wounded_man_to_safety_near_Boesinghe_on_1_August_1917_during_the_Third_Battle_of_Ypres._Q5935.jpg

23 Photo zoomed in. https://commons.wikimedia.org/wiki/File:The_Battle_of_Cambrai,_November-december_1917_Q7287.jpg

24 https://commons.wikimedia.org/wiki/File:The_Second_Battle_of_the_Marne,_July-august_1918_Q6864.jpg

25 https://commons.wikimedia.org/wiki/File:Hannover_CL_IIIa_Argonnen_1918.JPEG

26 https://commons.wikimedia.org/wiki/File:RUSSIAN_COLD_STEEL_IN_EAST_PRUSSIA,_AUGUST_26th,_1914.png

27 Photo zoomed in. www.esercito.difesa.it, CC BY 2.5 <https://creativecommons.org/licenses/by/2.5>, via Wikimedia Commons: https://commons.wikimedia.org/wiki/File:WWI_-_Battle_of_the_Piave_River_-_Italian_machine_gun_position_near_Cand.jpg

28 Orjen, CC BY-SA 3.0 <http://creativecommons.org/licenses/by-sa/3.0/>, via Wikimedia Commons: https://commons.wikimedia.org/wiki/File:Jezerski_Vrh_(2694)_sa_Karanfila_(2480).jpg

29 Decora, CC BY-SA 2.5 <https://creativecommons.org/licenses/by-sa/2.5>, via Wikimedia Commons: https://commons.wikimedia.org/wiki/File:Russian_empire_sea_access_wwi.png

30 Harry Alonzo Chase, Public domain, via Wikimedia Commons: https://commons.wikimedia.org/wiki/File:T_E_Lawrence_1888-1935_Q73535.jpg

31 Photo zoomed in. https://commons.wikimedia.org/wiki/File:Wright_First_Flight_1903Dec17_(restore_115).tif?page=1

32 https://commons.wikimedia.org/wiki/File:Manfred_von_Richthofen.jpg

33 https://commons.wikimedia.org/wiki/File:Postcard_LZ_47_LZ_77_Luftschiff_Zeppelin.jpg

34 https://commons.wikimedia.org/wiki/File:Preparing_6-inch_AA_gun_Dover_WWI_IWM_Q_18281.jpg

35 Photo zoomed in. SMU Libraries Digital Collections, No restrictions, via Wikimedia Commons: https://commons.wikimedia.org/wiki/File:(German_U-boat_UB_14_with_its_crew).jpg

36 Luz28, CC0, via Wikimedia Commons: https://commons.wikimedia.org/wiki/File:WWI_Gas_Mask.png

37 Cassowary Colorizations, CC BY 2.0 <https://creativecommons.org/licenses/by/2.0>, via Wikimedia Commons: https://commons.wikimedia.org/wiki/File:Obergefreiter_with_a_Nebelhandgranate_Stielhandgranate_M-24_(37073699142).png

38 Photo zoomed in. National Library of Scotland, No restrictions, via Wikimedia Commons: https://commons.wikimedia.org/wiki/File:British_messenger_dogs_with_their_handler,_France,_during_World_War_I_(2957940591).jpg

39 Engraving by Norman Wilkinson, The Illustrated London News. Public Domain via Wikimedia: https://commons.wikimedia.org/wiki/File:Sinking_of_the_Lusitania_London_Illus_News.jpg

40 https://commons.wikimedia.org/wiki/File:Woodrow_Wilson,_Army-Navy_Game_1915.jpg

41 https://commons.wikimedia.org/wiki/File:U.S._Marines_-_active_service_-_land,_sea,_air_LCCN00652140.tif

42 https://commons.wikimedia.org/wiki/File:American_White_and_Negro_soldiers_being_served_to_chocolate_and_sandwich_rolls_in_canteen_established_in_basement_of_American_Red_Cross_Bureau_of_Refugees_at_Toulouse.jpg

43 Egrim21Egrim21, CC BY-SA 4.0 <https://creativecommons.org/licenses/by-sa/4.0>, via Wikimedia Commons: https://commons.wikimedia.org/wiki/File:Women_Navy_Recruit_Poster.jpg

44 Thought Co., Public domain, via Wikimedia Commons: https://commons.wikimedia.org/wiki/File:Renault_tanks_during_the_Battle_of_Saint-Mihiel.jpg

45 https://commons.wikimedia.org/wiki/File:Russian_peasants_LOC_16872467542.jpg

46 Dmitry Ilyich Leshchenko (1876–1937): Lenin. Collection Of Photographs And Stills in two volumes, vol. 1, Russian edition, Moscow, 1970: page 46, Public domain, via Wikimedia Commons: https://commons.wikimedia.org/wiki/File:Lenin-last-underground,_1917.jpg

47 https://commons.wikimedia.org/wiki/File:Revoluci%C3%B3n-marzo-rusia--russianbolshevik00rossuoft.png

48 https://commons.wikimedia.org/wiki/File:Russian_Imperial_Family_1913.jpg

49 Photo zoomed in. KcdKosova, CC BY-SA 3.0 <https://creativecommons.org/licenses/by-sa/3.0>, via Wikimedia Commons: https://commons.wikimedia.org/wiki/File:Balkans_map_selim_wikfianli.jpg

50 https://commons.wikimedia.org/wiki/File:Officers_celebrate_at_captured_German_canteen,_Cedar_Creek_%26_Belle_Grove_National_Historical_Park,_1918._(8b5a3fbd47b24e96a6c40a73f62f3ed7).jpg

51 Woodrow Wilson Presidential Library Archives, No restrictions, via Wikimedia Commons: https://commons.wikimedia.org/wiki/File:The_Big_Four,_Paris_peace_conference.jpg

52 Zoomed in, labels added. The.Modificator, Public domain, via Wikimedia Commons: https://commons.wikimedia.org/wiki/File:Europe_1920_simplyfied.svg

53 Labels added. Hoodinski, CC BY-SA 3.0 <https://creativecommons.org/licenses/by-sa/3.0>, via Wikimedia Commons: https://commons.wikimedia.org/wiki/File:Traktat_w_Trianon.svg

54 https://commons.wikimedia.org/wiki/File:Rauf_Orbay,_Kemal_Atat%C3%BCrk_and_R%C3%BCstem_Bilinski_at_the_Sivas_Congress_(1919).png

www.ingramcontent.com/pod-product-compliance
Lightning Source LLC
Chambersburg PA
CBHW070335010526
44107CB00004B/512